COUNTRY-STYLE STENCILING

COUNTRY-STYLE STENCILING

by MARGARET BOYLES

Line Drawings by Hope Eastman

Meredith® Press, New York

For Meredith® Press:

Director: Elizabeth P. Rice
Project Manager: Connie Schrader
Assistant: Ruth Weadock
Project Editor: Vivien Fauerbach
Proofs: Carol Anderson
Production Manager: Bill Rose
Photography by Margaret Boyles

ISBN: 0-696-02337-7
Library of Congress Card Number: 89-063581
Printed in the United States of America
10 9 8 7 6 5 4 3 2 1

ACKNOWLEDGMENTS

Instead of a formal acknowledgment, I should like to thank the wonderful family and friends who provided a great deal of help in the preparation of the manuscript for this book. I dedicate the book to all of them!

First, there is Barry, my husband, who never complained about projects that did not stay in the studio, late or skipped meals, a high school reunion and vacation that couldn't fit into the production schedule, paint under my fingernails and in my hair, the entire house turned upside down for photography sessions, and other indignities too numerous to list.

Hope, whose line drawings grace these pages, is the best help I have ever had! Always on time to meet deadlines with her perfect work, her interest, enthusiasm, and help with the project, she has made this one of the happiest projects I have ever undertaken.

There is really no way to express thanks to my dear friend and superb editor, Constance Schrader! After working with her for twenty years, I still find it incredible that I was lucky enough to have been chosen as one of "her" authors. She has been calm and helpful in every crisis, and always full of good ideas. I hope we have another twenty years in which to work together!

My precious little Meagan perhaps made the most sacrifices to getting the manuscript finished. We had to spend much less time together than we like, but we truly enjoyed every minute we did find. She learned to sand, paint, and stencil. When I couldn't make a tulip look as though a little girl had drawn it, she drew it for me! I thank her for that design—and for her little cabinet, which she helped paint and really did stencil with those perfect floral sprays! I am the luckiest of all grandmothers!

My sister, Pat, is a talented lady I call on for all kinds of help. She always responds quickly. We had lots of ideas for designs we didn't have space for, but there is always another book coming for which I hope she'll have time to be here in the studio!

There are so many others: My dear "Captain" Jack, who made the Shaker hanging rack, my favorite project; and the staff at Meredith Press. I thank them all!

TABLE OF CONTENTS

Dear Stencil-Crafter:

The craft of stenciling has a beautiful, rich past: Americans have used stencil designs to bring color and beauty to their homes since Colonial times. Stenciling patterns have also been used for centuries throughout the world.

With Margaret Boyles' clear and easy-to-follow directions, and her uniquely appealing and graceful designs, you can transform ordinary fabric, paper, wood, metal, and ceramic objects into one-of-a-kind accents for every room in your home. From charming pastel soft-stencils—such as the *Rose of Sharon Quilt*—to a classic *Sacherville Trunk* highlighted by a glowing golden Fleur-de-Lis motif, full-size, ready-to-trace stencil designs invite you to enjoy this timeless craft.

We at Meredith are very proud of the craft books we publish. They are of the highest quality and offer projects for every level of crafting skill. Our books feature large, full-color photographs of all projects, as well as instructions and charts that are simple and readable. *COUNTRY-STYLE STENCILING* also includes color art to guide you in shading the designs. The projects cover a wide range of design styles and uses.

We hope you'll use *COUNTRY-STYLE STENCILING* with pleasure—and that you'll be as proud of your creations as we are of ours.

Connie Schrader

CONNIE SCHRADER
Editorial Project Manager

INTRODUCTION

There's magic in a stencil—an unassuming piece of film or paper with a pattern cut into it. Holding a stencil in one's hand makes it easy to remember the first simple example we discovered as children and the wonder of being able to draw the same image over and over again. Then, in addition, being able to add color: to make one red image, one blue—that was really discovery!

The stencil has been a sophisticated and valuable decorating tool for thousands of years. We read that Roman boys were taught to write using a stylus and stencil. In a French church there are stenciled designs dating from the fifteenth century that are not unlike our geometrics. In fact, at that time stencils were used all over Europe as well as in the Orient, where opulent silk kimonos and obis were decorated with elegant stenciling.

Perhaps of greatest interest to those of us who love today's country-style decorating are the stencils of the eighteenth-century New England itinerant stencilers. Entire rooms showcasing their artistry have been preserved. Perhaps the best known of these itinerants is Moses Eaton, who decorated many homes in return for room and board and sometimes a small stipend. He mixed his own paints and cut metal stencils of his vibrant and enduring designs.

How different things are for us today—paints in myriad colors, the best brushes, books of inspiring designs, even stencils cut by laser, are available. All this has made it possible to add to the repertoire of designs, even to change basic stencils to eliminate the connecting pieces known as bridges and to create a completely new look. We now stencil the walls of a room to match the pattern of a bright chintz, often adding custom stencils and matching pillows and small accessories to repeat the design or tie everything together. Moses really would be excited.

Moses also would enjoy our attachment to country-style decorating, which has roots in his own time. He would love the bright, uncluttered interiors, country-primitive furniture, old paintings, and accessories accented with stenciled patterns. This elegant new approach to country decorating has inspired the designs in this book. They range from a pure classic Greek Key design to country flowers and adaptations of folk art. Colors are as varied as styles to facilitate use in many interiors and as inspiration. For purposes of illustration, we have selected certain designs for specific projects, but all of our designs can be adapted to many different uses. Imagine the flowing swag that is shown on the Country Garden shelf enlarged slightly and painted along the ceiling of a country bedroom. A big blue bow could be added where the repeats join to add sunshine to a little girl's heart.

Working the patterns for this book has been a joy for me. No, my home is not completely covered with stenciling, but there is a bedroom, a downstairs service hall, and lots of interesting little boxes decorated with this favorite art of mine. Stenciling is a creative craft that is easy to fall in love with: One idea leads to another, and one finds that there is never enough time for the many possibilities that come to mind.

Remember, too, that children love to stencil. They have such fun. Today's new paints make cleanup easy. Seven-year-old Meagan wanted the little white cabinet as soon as she saw it unpacked, and she was so pleased when she was allowed to stencil it for this

book. Her work is as perfect as any adult's, and now her career as a stenciler is launched. But children can also be inspired by projects that are less elegant than the little cabinet. Give them some paint and let them make greeting cards, gift wrapping, or little gift boxes.

Of the several styles of stencils in this book, some are the traditional one-piece designs with bridges; others are a little different in that the design is created by successive layers without bridges. Also, some of the designs have been outlined in black ink to simulate Pennsylvania Dutch Fraktur art, and some have small details added with permanent markers. These details make the book special for me, and I hope they are ideas that you will use and enjoy!

—MARGARET BOYLES

THE BASICS

THE BASICS

The art of stenciling is easy to learn, inexpensive and, most of all, very satisfying. The few basic materials required can readily be found in crafts, art supply, and hardware stores, and substitutes often can be used very satisfactorily. In this section of the book, supplies will be discussed, cutting and making stencils will be explained, and painting techniques will be demonstrated. After reading this material, you will be able to start work on anything from a sheet of gaily printed wrapping paper to the floors and walls of a charming country room.

MATERIALS AND EQUIPMENT

Paints

Moses Eaton, the well-known New England itinerant stenciler, mixed his own buttermilk paint and probably tinted it with chemicals from the kitchen or garden. Today one has only to decide which paint is best suited for the project at hand. There are many colors to delight and excite, and the range available by mixing one's own colors is endless. With paints intended for hard surfaces and paints especially formulated for fabric, finding just the right color for the type of surface on which you wish to work is a pleasant task.

Acrylic or Latex Stencil Paints: These paints, sold in one- and two-ounce containers in a wide range of colors, have been formulated to the proper consistency for dry-brush stenciling. They dry quickly and can be cleaned up with water. The colors are wonderful and can be intermixed for special, subtle variations of tone and hue. When dry, these paints are washable. They may be used on all surfaces, including wood, fabric, and walls. For best results when using these paints on fabric, combine them with a water-based textile medium. This will greatly improve their performance on an absorbent surface and preserve the softness of the fabric.

For those who hesitate to combine colors themselves, the makers of many of these acrylic stencil paints package small containers in coordinated sets. There is a box of all brights, including the primaries; a pastel set; and a palette of the most popular country colors. Such sets provide an economical way to begin stenciling.

Stencil Paint Sticks or Crayons: This unique new product combines linseed oil and pigment in a compressed wax base. For beginners it is the most mistake-proof paint available. Not only is it easy to use, it is fun! The color is applied to the stencil itself, then brushed onto the surface to be colored, making very delicate shading easy. A true oil paint, in a wide range of colors, it will dry overnight, and it is sufficiently smudge-proof to allow successive colors to be placed next to paint which has just been applied. There is no mess, no odor. The new brush cleaners allow cleanup with soap and water, but turpentine or mineral spirits also may be used.

Two well-known brands of these paints in stick form are available at present. Both perform as well on wood as on fabric. Many of the color prints of designs shown in this book have been worked with these versatile paints.

Japan Paints: These are an excellent choice when a fast-drying, oil-based paint is needed.

The japan formula dries almost instantly, thus preventing paint from seeping under the stencil or smearing when subsequent colors are added. Although the range of colors is not extremely wide, this paint may be mixed to customize designs. Japan paint has a translucent glow different from that obtainable with any other paint. A glance at the brilliance of the stenciled apples on the Candle Box on page 40 will illustrate this beautifully.

As for any other oil-based paints, cleaning up with turpentine or mineral spirits is recommended.

Spray Paints: Although spray paints take some practice to apply effectively and a great deal of masking to prevent overspray, wonderful effects can be achieved with them. Colors are good, and there is a choice of latex or oil-based paint as well as lacquer. For metallic effects, sprays packaged for automobile touch-ups are especially effective.

The interesting textures that can be created with sprays result from the fact that spray paint is dispensed as very tiny droplets which build up to cover a surface. A lightly sprayed surface makes this texture more apparent and is sometimes more desirable than a flat-coated area.

Household Paint Products: Many stencilers use latex paints and oil-based paints intended for household use and produce lovely results. The obvious advantage is cost and availability. The dry-brush method works well with these paints and when the project is large, this alternative should be considered.

Artist's Paints: Either oil or acrylic paints in tubes work very well for stenciling. Both mix and blend well and are permanent when dry. One disadvantage is that time must be allowed for drying before a second color is added.

Fabric Dyes: Because fabric dyes are absorbed into the fibers of a material rather than sitting on top of it, as is true of most paints, dyes, once they are set, generally are more permanent than paints. There are many dye formulas available, most of which leave the fabric soft and pliable. To ensure color fastness, always wash the fabric before stenciling, and carefully follow the dye maker's instructions for setting the color.

Stencils

One of the main components of Moses Eaton's stencil equipment, still intact in his carrying box, is his collection of metal stencils. Cutting these must have required a great deal of skill, but using them must also have been difficult as it was impossible to see through the metal to check registration. Today's materials are so much easier to use, and they produce results which are just as beautiful.

The best material from which to cut a stencil is mylar or acetate film in a gauge heavy enough to make the stencil reusable. Mylar or acetate can be bought in crafts and art supply stores in pads, sheets, or rolls. The best weight is 5-millimeter, but if this is unavailable, 3-millimeter gauge can be substituted. Although the lighter-weight material will not be quite as sturdy, it will last long enough to allow completion of most projects.

Especially good are stencil blanks packaged by the stencil paint companies. These are usually a good quality 5-millimeter-weight mylar, which is easy to cut and strong enough to be used many times. Another good product is the oversized stencil blanks made especially for borders and marked with permanent guidelines.

Many, many already-cut stencils, well designed and ready to use, may also be bought. These are usually dye- or laser-cut to ensure absolutely smooth edges. Wonderful time-savers, these stencils produce perfect results and are often a quick solution to design problems.

Although stencils can be cut from many different types of paper, paper stencils wear out quickly and are not sufficiently transparent to allow easy placement of succeeding overlays.

Brushes

The stencil brush, a brush designed especially for stenciling, is a stubby brush with blunt-cut bristles. Made to hold small amounts of paint, it can be purchased with either natural or synthetic bristles in a variety of sizes. It is good to have a selection on hand to meet needs for different sizes and to provide a brush for each color that will be used.

Clean, well-cared-for brushes will last a long time. Follow the paint manufacturer's instructions for cleanup after each use, and store the brushes so the bristles do not bear the weight of the handles.

Mineral spirits, turpentine, specially formulated brush cleaners, and water are all excellent cleaners, depending upon the kind of paint used. The odorless gel-like brush cleaners, which sometimes remove what seems like hopelessly dried paint from a brush, are very handy. (They sometimes even remove dried paint from clothing!)

No matter which cleaner is used, always finishing with soap and water usually leaves the brush in better condition. Shake out excess water, blot with a towel, and shape the bristles into their original form. If, after much usage, the bristles begin to flare out, wrap a rubber band around them while wet and allow them to dry.

Also handy for applying paint are little square sponges made in three layers so that the top layer folds back to become a handle. These sponges can be used for applying antiquing solution or small amounts of paint. Cleanup with soap and water or turpentine is easy, but because the sponges are so inexpensive it is not extravagant to dispose of them after use.

Other Equipment

The various paints or fabric dyes required for every project in this book are listed under *Materials* in the blue-tinted box shown with each project.

In addition to these special supplies, which give character and uniqueness to each design, the stenciler also needs a collection of standard equipment—basics as fundamental as tracing paper and pencil, for example, without which no stenciling can be done.

For your convenience, these standard supplies are listed in the blue-tinted box on page 16. Before you start work on any project, refer to these blue-tinted boxes as you would to a checklist to be sure that everything you need is assembled on your worktable, ready for use.

An inexpensive *artist's knife*, usually called an X-Acto knife, with interchangeable blades is the best tool for cutting mylar for a stencil. Buy a selection of blades and always work with a new one to ensure easy cutting and clean edges. Try several different shapes. Some stencilers find the basic sharp point best; others prefer a curved blade.

Use a plastic *cutting board*, heavy cardboard, or a self-healing, rubberlike cutting surface to protect the surface on which the stencil is to be cut. A small cutting mat is convenient because it allows the whole design to be rotated while cutting. A 12″ × 12″ mat is a practical size unless the design is very large.

Using *spray adhesive* on the back of the stencil will hold it firmly in place while it is painted and will prevent most smearing and run-unders. Spray sparingly and allow the adhesive to sit a few minutes. The stencil can then be moved easily and repositioned many times without additional spraying.

The disadvantage of using the spray is that the adhesive must be removed before the stencil can be turned over to make a reverse image. Solve this problem by cutting an entire design, including the portion that you wish to reverse. Then spray the entire back.

Although many adhesives are marketed just for stenciling, a good artist's mounting spray is all that is needed.

The adhesive on *drafting tape* makes it much better than masking tape for use with stencils. A new white tape which uses the same kind of adhesive as is used on the ubiquitous little yellow notes we all love is very good for stencil placement. It holds firmly, but does not lift off paint when it is removed. This tape is also handy for blocking off little open areas when two colors are used close together.

The Basics

Purchase a *draftsman's pen* with permanent ink for use in tracing designs onto film. These pens are available in many thicknesses and usually contain ink and a nib which facilitate tracing on mylar. Laundry markers and felt-tip pens with a fine point also can be used on film.

Permanent felt-tip pens or markers can be used to add such details as veins in leaves or to outline entire stenciled designs to simulate early Fraktur art, as has been done on some of the designs in this book. For tiny lines and other intricate work, a pen is much easier to control than a brush.

Many different kinds of *fabrics* can be used for stenciling. For quilting, clothing, and household items, use 100 percent cotton or a blend of cotton and polyester. Use either solid colors or small prints. Before stenciling any fabric, check the paint label to make sure that particular paint is colorfast on the fabric you've selected: Some paints are best on 100 percent cotton and others work best on a blend of cotton and polyester. Wash all fabric before stenciling to remove the sizing. Otherwise the paint will sit on top of the sizing and wash off when the sizing is removed in the first washing.

Fabric markers are essential tools if small details are to be added to stenciled designs on fabric. Several brands are available. Be sure to buy markers with permanent ink.

TRACING AND CUTTING STENCILS

Most of the stencil designs shown in this book have been produced full-size, ready for tracing and immediate use. Many also have been reproduced in color. These color prints illustrate color and shading, and I hope they also will provide creative inspiration.

A black-and-white drawing accompanies each project. As noted, most drawings are presented full-size. If this is not the case, the instructions for the project direct that the design be reduced or enlarged by photocopy machine. To make cutting and separating colors for stencil overlays easy, a Color Key is provided for each project. The corresponding color numbers on the various color elements of the design indicate each overlay to be cut. The instructions for each project further explain how to make the overlays.

Stencils which are one-color patterns require only one stencil and therefore do not have color keys or numbers.

In preparation for cutting stencil overlays

for a project, make a copy or a tracing of the design as shown below. (Please note that because a copy machine usually distorts a design slightly, a tracing will actually be more accurate.)

Using the Color Key and color pencils or crayons, fill in the tracing with the colors indicated by the numbers in the **Color Key**. These numbers indicate that the bow is to be colored two shades of blue, the leaves and flower calyxes green, the flowers rose. The finished page should look like the Country Pinks Pillow stencil shown here.

Place the stencil film over the colored copy and, using a marker or pen with permanent ink, trace all of the areas indicated by a

Country Pinks Pillow Stencil, traced and colored with pencils.

single color. There should be as many stencils as there are colors on the tracing. Thus four separate stencils should be cut—one for each shade of blue, one for the rose, and one for the green. The instructions for the project indicate that the two blue stencils will be painted using the same color blue. This method of separating the elements of a stencil allows one to paint a very natural kind of stencil design. With this method of overlapping stencils, it is important to be especially accurate in tracing the portions of design that lie next to each other.

When a single fine line such as a flower stem is shown on the drawing, draw the fine line on the stencil film. Then, when cutting the stencil, cut a fine line by running the knife along each side of the drawn line.

If the stencil film has a frosted side and a glossy side, trace and paint on the glossy side. Allow enough extra space on the stencil so the paint won't smear beyond the edges and to add extra strength to the stencil. If space is tight and cutting close to the edge is necessary, tape or slide a piece of paper along the edge to catch any overlapping paint.

Use an X-Acto knife with a new, sharp blade for cutting. The blade may be either pointed or curved. Try both to see which works best. Change blades often!

A small cutting mat—about 12″ × 12″, as described earlier—is a big help in cutting. Place the film right side up on the mat. *Cut small areas first.* Control is best when you cut by pulling the knife toward you. Apply pressure evenly and just heavily enough to cut through the mylar. Applying too much pressure is a common beginner problem that causes the hand and arm to tire quickly. Cut only until tired; rest, then resume. The cutting pro-

cess should be enjoyable, and, as skill develops, one that will take little time.

When cutting a curve, insert the knife and begin moving along the curve, turning the entire mat rather than the knife and trying not to interrupt the flow of the line by removing the knife. This is where the small mat is a big help because it can be turned with a slow, even motion.

Try to stay on the cutting lines as much as possible. Don't worry about tiny irregularities in cutting. These give the painted work a much softer, more informal look, which is often preferred by professional stencilers.

When the stencils have been cut, place them face up on a clean paper towel, and remove any remaining ink with a damp, soapy towel. If the ink is truly permanent, it won't rub off. If it is washable, it will be removed before it can be carried into the paint when the stenciling is done and produce a muddy, gray color.

Changing the Size of a Design

It is no longer necessary to go through the old process of drawing a design onto inch-square grids and hoping the enlargement will be a fairly good reproduction of the original. A copy machine in your local shopping center or stationery store will enlarge or reduce a design in moments and produce a fairly accurate replica of the original. While an effort has been made to make every design in this book full-size and ready for tracing, you may wish at times to adjust the size of a design so that it can be used on something entirely different from the object shown in this book.

If this is the case, measure the length or width of the original design and determine the size of the reproduction. In most photocopy shops, the operator will be able to figure the needed adjustment, either on his machine or by using a proportional scale. If the copier is a self-service machine, estimate the required enlargement or reduction and make one copy as a basis for calculating any further adjustments.

PREPARATION OF SURFACES

All surfaces to be stenciled must be clean and dry. This rule applies to everything—walls, paint, new wood, metal, paper, baskets, and anything else. Base coats of paint may be latex or oil; a satin or flat finish is best.

Although stenciled designs are usually pictured on pale—white, buff or eggshell—backgrounds, deep, rich colors can also be very effective bases for this art. Wallpaper with a texture or small print can also provide an interesting background, for a faint outline of the print usually shows through the stencil paint, thus adding additional texture. The designs in this book have been painted on paper of various textures and colors to illustrate the different effects that can be achieved by using different kinds of surfaces for stenciling. In the picture of the Candle Box (page 40), notice the difference in brightness and texture in the apples painted with japan paint or natural wood and the apples painted with stencil crayon on paper for the wall border. Both are beautiful—just different!

Most of the attractive wood pieces in this book were new and arrived neatly sealed in shrink-wrap plastic, ready to be finished. They needed only a little touch-up sanding before the paint or stain was applied. A coat of alcohol-based white primer was all that was needed as an undercoat for either oil or acrylic

background colors. The flat finish of the "folk art" base coats takes stencil paint very well. As a final touch, several layers of glaze coat will protect the stenciling and add gloss if desired, and a flat sealer will provide protection without producing a shine.

Walls should be in good shape before stenciling commences. Investing in a new coat of paint is worthwhile, since the stenciling will last a long time and it would be a shame to apply it to a dingy background.

Flat latex is a very good base coat for a stenciled wall, but oil-based paint is also good. While it is generally recommended that flat or satin finishes be used for best results, good prints can be achieved on glossy surfaces by applying the stencil pattern with spray paint.

Metal surfaces to be stenciled must be primed and sealed. There are special products for this purpose. Stencil metal with acrylic or oil paints and protect with sealer. Although metal surfaces do chip easily and should not be subjected to prolonged exposure to water, decorative items thus protected will last many years with good care. Much early stenciling was done on metal, particularly tin, and is highly prized.

PAINTING A STENCIL

Now that the paints and other materials have been assembled, the stencil is cut and the surface is prepared, it is time to start painting a stencil! But before you apply paint to your project, take a few minutes to make a practice print on scrap paper. Sometimes paints which look wonderful sitting beside each other in their containers look absolutely terrible when applied to a flat surface. Practicing also gives you a chance to see how the layers of overlays work together and which order of painting achieves the best registration.

Once your are satisfied with your practice prints, spray the backs of the stencil overlays with adhesive and position the first stencil for painting.

The dry-brush method is the best for most purposes. Begin by placing a small amount of stencil paint in a flat saucer or on a paper plate (the little plastic lids from "deli" containers are also ideal).

Holding the brush upright, dip the tips of the bristles into the color. Work in a circular motion on a paper towel until the color seems to be dry and no little circular dark marks appear. Repeat this process. Now the brush is ready for painting.

In stenciling, as in embroidery or handwriting, the individuality of each artist will be apparent. However, best results will be obtained by using a very light circular motion, with the brush held in the upright position shown. This prevents paint from running under the stencil film and allows for either an even coat or shading.

Stenciling techniques vary. Some people prefer an even coat of paint; others like to apply the paint heavily at the edges and blend to almost nothing at the center to create an illu-

Painting a Stencil

sion of depth. Still other people like to add shading with additional paint. Develop your own style as you learn.

Most paints allow the stencil for one color to be lifted and the second color to be applied immediately, without worry about smearing. If you make a mistake, or if paint seeps under the stencil, don't fret. Use a little background paint and a sharp watercolor brush to touch up and no one, probably including yourself, will notice after the paint is dry.

When using stencil crayons, the easiest medium in which to work, the method is slightly different. Position the stencil, then apply the crayon on the film around the cut edges of the stencil. Rub the brush into the paint in a circular motion and pull it into the cut-out areas. Color may be built up until the desired depth is achieved. Stencil crayons make it very easy to shade by working heavier at the edges and leaving background showing in the middle.

Shading may also be done by blending in another color. A leaf can often be enhanced when it is first painted green and then a bit of blue is added close to the base and blended in. Yellow can also be worked into the tip of the leaf.

The pretty shading in the flowers on the Country Pinks Pillow (page 68) was achieved by first painting the entire flower pink, then blending in a tiny bit of rose at the base of the flower.

Some of the color prints in this book have been embellished by the addition of a fine, black, broken outline, simulating the appearance of some of the old Pennsylvania Dutch Fraktur art. The black outline brings colors forward visually. This is an effective technique and is something you might want to try.

Another attractive technique that can be seen in some of the stencil designs is the use of permanent markers with fine points to add stems and veins in leaves freehand. These delicate additions have a softening effect and, in some cases, save a great deal of time that otherwise would have been spent cutting stencils.

Keep in mind that working on a background of flat-finish paint allows the stencil paints to adhere well. After your stencil painting is dry, you may wish to apply a protective coat of varnish or sealer to add a high gloss or preserve the matte finish.

Clean your stencils after use and store them flat. A manila folder makes a good storage container, and interleaving the stencils with wax paper will prevent the collection from sticking together in case all the adhesive or paint was not removed.

SPECIAL FINISHES

Metallic Paints

There is something particularly appealing about a painted piece accented with a touch of gold or silver. Today's paint products make adding these touches possible with little practice.

A very easily applied metallic is a wax paste that adds the glow of a precious metal to many surfaces when rubbed on with a fingertip or a soft cloth. The same paste may be thinned with mineral spirits or turpentine and applied with a brush on larger areas. It is also very pretty used just as a highlight. Among the many colors available are classic gold, white gold, red gold, silver, copper, and brass. The finish obtained with this gilding should be protected with a clear spray with either a glossy or matte finish.

Metallic Paints

Using spray paint is a favorite and quick method of applying a metallic finish. Spray paints sold in crafts stores and intended for this particular use seem to be brighter and stay bright longer than others. Of course, surfaces not to be gilded will have to be masked, but the speed of the painting process is so great that the time spent in masking is worthwhile. A final spray of clear sealer or glaze coat will prevent tarnishing.

The third option for adding metallic finish is gold leaf powder. Many shades are available. The powder should be mixed with clear varnish to make a thick but brushable liquid. Spoon a small amount of the powder into a small dish or other container. Then add very small amounts of varnish, stirring to mix. Always add the liquid to the powder to prevent lumps.

Although metallic finishes stay bright for a long time, they are best protected by a clear coating of varnish.

Antiquing

There is no need to wait years for time to create that wonderful patina on prized antiques and collectibles! Antiquing will accomplish this feat in minutes. This process is very fast, and it is forgiving enough to let a novice try with assured success. But before you begin, here is a convenient way to practice: Keep a small piece of scrap wood on the worktable and, before cleaning the brush for use with another color, paint the scrap with each successive coat of paint or finish you have used on the project. Then, when the time comes to experiment with applying an antiquing solution, a practice piece is ready to test the color and technique.

Surfaces to be antiqued must be sealed first. New wood needs a coat of sealer. Older projects being refinished are probably already painted or varnished and will probably not need the sealer coat.

Reading the instructions for some of the projects in this book and noting that colors like bright aqua, barn red, and pimento are used might be a bit startling at first, but when one looks at the effects created by antiquing these colors, it is apparent that antiquing is a very versatile and beautiful technique. The solution adds beautiful depth and age.

If you use a water-based antiquing solution, which can be found in a variety of colors

Antiquing

in crafts stores, merely follow the instructions on the package. Most water-based solutions must be applied with a little sponge or sponge brush, and then wiped to add highlighting.

Create additional colors with mixtures of equal parts of acrylic base coat or stencil paints and extender. Good colors to use are black, burnt umber, dark green, and dark blue, depending upon the needs of the project at hand. For example, when the colors of the stenciled design on the Small Trunk with Country Tile Lid (page 125) seemed too bright, a thin solution using yellow ocher as coloring agent was used sparingly to soften the contrast.

If you prefer not to use a commercially prepared solution, use the traditional antiquing solution of a mixture of equal parts of oil pigment, mineral spirits, and boiled linseed oil. This mixture is slower to dry and thus allows more working time to perfect shading, but be sure to use *boiled* linseed oil, or it will be tacky forever!

Whatever kind of antiquing solution you decide to use, start by painting the entire piece with the solution. Allow it to dry until it begins to feel tacky. Then, with a soft, lint-free cloth, rub off the color in the areas where it would have worn off naturally through constant use. Highlight the areas that would not be very worn. To add the impression of age, you might also obscure parts of the edges of the stenciled pattern. Sometimes adding a bit of "fly specking," especially on stenciled areas, after the antiquing solution has been applied will provide a further illusion of age.

Pickling

Pickling, another name for antiquing, is generally done by applying white or pale colors in a thin coat and rubbing them off to allow the wood grain to show. Like the solutions for antiquing, products for pickling come in many colors, may be bought in crafts stores, and can easily be mixed from equal parts of extender and paint. White is the favorite color, but pastels add a soft glow. Most of the commercially prepared pickling solutions are water-based and dry quickly.

Mix an oil-based pickling solution from equal portions of oil pigment, mineral spirits, and boiled linseed oil. As in traditional antiquing, the wood must be sealed with a coat of varnish before the pickling mixture is applied to the entire piece. Use a soft, lint-free rag to highlight the grain of the wood. The oil-based formula allows plenty of time to perfect the application.

Pickling

Faux Tortoiseshell

There is no way to be interested in stenciling without developing an interest in, or at least a curiosity about the faux paint finishes that have been used with stenciling for hundreds of years. Tortoiseshell is one of the most beautiful and is surprisingly easy if one accepts a faux paint finish as an imitation and not as an attempt to re-create the real thing.

Experiment with this finish by practicing on a heavy white poster board which has been primed with two coats of white alcohol-based primer sealer or flat white latex paint. The base for tortoiseshell may be either a bright yellow or a metallic gold. The step-by-step example given here is yellow-based, and the Octagonal Clock on page 97 is worked over gold metallic paint. In each case, the coloring of the finished work is slightly different.

Before you begin working with this finish, be sure that the background paint is thoroughly dry. Then follow the steps listed beside the painted sample. Relax and enjoy this process. If the finished results are not pleasing, start over. A painted piece can't be ruined because it can always be painted again.

Faux Tortoiseshell

STEPS

Begin with a flat painted background, either bright yellow or metallic gold. Here bright yellow shows under the dark stain in the upper section.

1. Using the 1″ brush, apply a coat of the dark varnish over the yellow background. Work quickly and don't worry about the smoothness of coverage.

2. With the brush, make wavy strokes in the wet varnish, working on the diagonal as shown.

3. Thin a small amount of burnt·umber oil paint with a little mineral spirits. Using a small brush, such as a 14 watercolor brush, place free-form marks in and under the diagonal dark varnish markings.

4. Next, thin a little bit of black oil paint and put a very few scattered patches randomly in both dark and light areas.

5. If necessary, pick up excess paint by dabbing with a clean rag.

6. Using a clean, dry brush, stroke the entire piece diagonally, first in one direction, then in the other. The markings will begin to appear. Keep a clean rag close by and wipe the brush after stroking in one direction. The brush should remain truly dry.

7. When almost satisfied with the results, dip a clean watercolor brush into clean mineral spirits and randomly drop small amounts on your work surface. The solvent will spread, revealing some areas of background color. Dab with a clean rag if there is too much spreading. Note the three small yellow spots marked "7". These have just been dropped and spread. Compare these spots to those below, which have been brushed.

8. Add a little more mineral spirits to the black mixture. Dip a toothbrush into this mixture and gently spatter little specks in selected areas. Dry overnight.

9. Finish with clear varnish. Five or six coats are generally enough to add beautiful depth, but follow your own instincts to judge the exact number of coats necessary. This will be determined by the consistency of the varnish itself as well as by the thickness of the coat. Beginning after the third coat to avoid damage to the paint, rub very gently with steel wool after each successive coat.

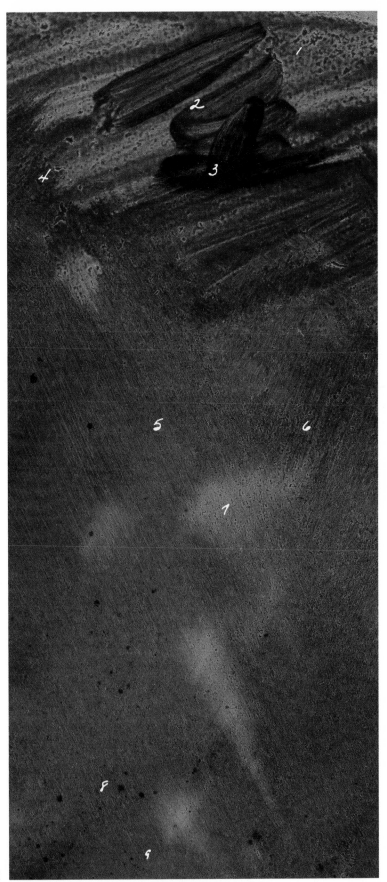

Print of Tortoiseshell

Sponging

Sponging is one of the easiest of the fancy paint finishes. A little exploration will reveal its many interesting effects and applications. Sponging entails applying two colors to a background of another color. Do not use more than two colors, for the design can easily become too busy and spoil the elegant effect. Practice using different colors and sponges on the white primed boards described for Tortoiseshelling (page 24).

Sponging

This sample of the sponging technique was made with a small marine sponge on a white low-gloss latex background. The sponging mixture was made from the two shades of blue used on the Tulip Flower Pots (page 50) mixed with extender and thickener. The fine texture of the sponge used here created a small pattern. Cellulose and more coarsely grained natural sponges will create slightly different patterns.

Follow the steps and pictures, and take time to develop a pleasing rhythm and pattern before you begin to work on the actual project.

(page 24).

Materials
White primed board or other
  surface on which to work
Flat base-coat paint
Two colors of paint for
  accenting
Extender
Thickener
Small sponge—a natural or
  marine sponge, if possible.
  If you use a cellulose
  sponge, tear it into an ir-
  regular, rounded shape.
  Pull out little pieces of
  sponge on one surface to
  ensure an uneven imprint.
Clear sealer, either matte or
  high-gloss finish

Remember that the background paint should be thoroughly dry before you start.

1. In a small flat saucer or dish, swirl a small amount of the secondary accent color. Follow this with a swirl of the most important accent color and equal amounts of extender and thickener. Tilt and rotate the dish slightly to cause the ingredients to run together.

2. Wet a small sponge in water. Wring as dry as possible. Dip the sponge in the paint mixture and dab repeatedly on paper, noticing the pattern and color mixture. Notice that the pattern becomes more pleasing as the sponge becomes drier. This is the time to begin applying the color to the board or project. Work lightly and in a random rather than a regularly spaced pattern. Dry well, then coat with varnish or clear sealer.

The Collection of Small Borders

Little details like the borders on pp. 28–29 can be the finishing touch for a very special project. Trace the parallel outlines of each design and the several repeats for each motif shown. Then color the tracing and cut a stencil overlay for each color shown. Trace the parallel outlines onto each overlay as guides for placement.

SUPPLIERS

Wood Products, Fabric, Lace

Retail

Margaret and Company
200 Wedgeway
Atlanta, GA 30350

Paints and All Other Stencil Equipment

The Stenciller's Emporium
P.O. Box 6039
Hudson, OH 44236

Wholesale

Write to the following wholesalers for retail suppliers in your area.

Plaid Enterprises, Inc.
P.O. Box 7600
Norcross, GA 30091

Yarn Tree Designs
P.O. Box 724
Ames, IA 50010

Stencil Ease
P.O. Box 282
Lincoln, RI 02865

Niji
Yasutomo and Company
235 Valley Drive
Brisbane, CA 94005

Walnut Hollow Farm
Rt. 2
Dodgeville, WI 53533

Charles Craft, Inc.
P.O. Box 1049
Laurinburg, NC 28352

Wichelt Imports, Inc.
Rt. 1
Stoddard, WI 54658

Tulip Productions
180 Elm Street
Waltham, MA 02254

The author and Meredith® Press thank these suppliers for their assistance.

BORDERS
1. Oriental Flower
2. Hearts
3. Geometric
4. Rosebud
5. Diamonds
6. Lancaster
7. Quilt
8. Sacherville
9. Colonial
10. Buttercup
11. Beading
12. Scallops
13. Ovals
14. Greek Key

Borders

GLOSSARY OF STENCILING TERMS

Antiquing. A process in which a dark color is brushed over the base color and rubbed to create the appearance of age.

Antiquing Solution. A mixture of pigment and a thinning agent used to add the look of gentle aging.

Bridge. A small portion of a stencil which connects one design element with the next in a running pattern.

Extender. A clear liquid medium mixed with acrylic paints to add drying time and transparency.

Glaze. A protective, lacquerlike, sprayed finish that builds up a thick, high-gloss coat, adding depth as well as protection to the design.

Linseed Oil. A drying oil extracted from flaxseed and used in making oil paints. For the projects in this book, use only boiled linseed oil.

Matte Finish. A sealed protective finish without a gloss.

Overlay. A stencil cut for use with just one color of a design. Successive layers of overlays allow colors to be placed adjacent to each other and permit better shading and freedom from bridges.

Pickling. An antiquing process usually worked over sealed natural wood with a white antiquing solution.

Print. A painted image made with the use of a stencil.

Registration Marks. Marks or portions of design reproduced on a stencil to indicate the precise alignment of successive overlays, thus ensuring a perfect print.

Shading. The technique of painting a design more heavily around the edges of the stencil to create delicate gradations of color.

Sponging. A traditional paint finish obtained by applying a number of different colors over a base coat with a small sponge.

Squeezing. A method of shortening a design, as for a border, to make it fit a specific area.

Stencil. A thin sheet of film, paper, or metal into which a pattern is cut so that, when paint or ink is applied to the opening, an image of the pattern is created.

Stretching. A method of lengthening a design to fit; the opposite of squeezing.

Textile Medium. A clear liquid which, when mixed with stencil paints, allows the paint to penetrate the fibers of textiles. This method of making the stencil paints suitable for use on fabric also leaves the fabric soft and pliable, the colors fast.

Thickener. A clear liquid which thickens acrylic paints and makes them more transparent.

COUNTRY GARDEN

COUNTRY GARDEN SHELF

INSTRUCTIONS

Pretty, bright pastels on a pristine, white shelf bring the cheerful beauty of a garden indoors, even though the flowers themselves are pure fancy. The long, repeating design may be shortened or lengthened to fit any requirement. Enlarged slightly, it would be lovely as a border around the ceiling of a room or above a chair rail. The center section is shown in the print and on one of the cards on page 11.

Review checklist (page 16) and assemble all basic stenciling supplies. Review the materials list for this project (page 35).

Sand and prepare the wood for painting (see "The Basics," page 19). Apply white primer-sealer and several coats of the white base coat. Dry thoroughly.

Trace the center section of the stencil design (page 34). Add the side section (page 32) and the side end section (page 34), joining each at the overlap shown by the broken lines on the drawings. Using the Color Key and the numbers on the drawings, color the tracing as instructed on page 16 in "The Basics." Cut one stencil for each color indicated on the drawings. Placing the suggested colors where shown

Side Section Stencil for Country Garden Shelf (Color Key, page 34)

Country Garden Shelf

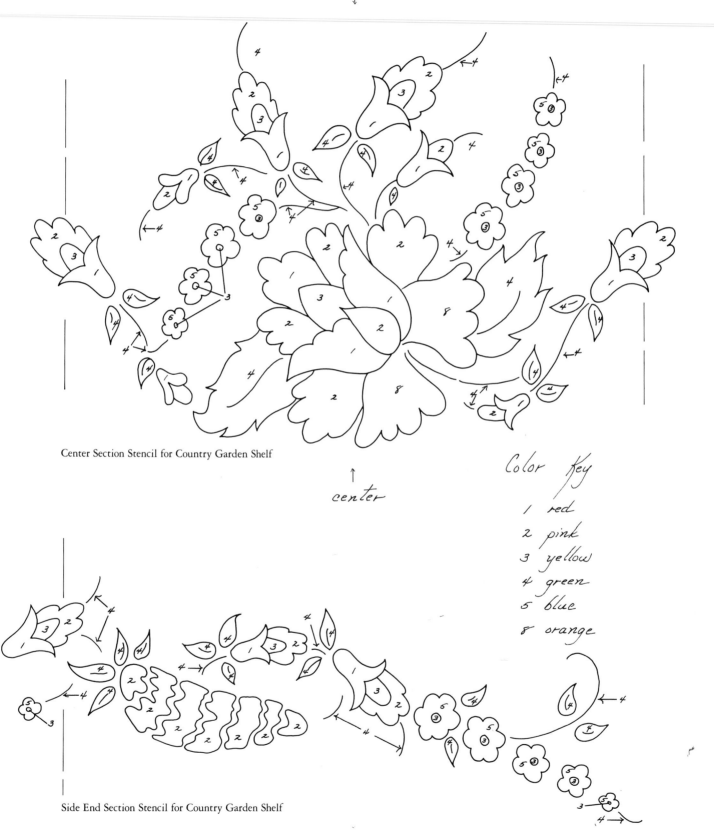

center
↓

Center Section Stencil for Country Garden Shelf

↑
center

Color Key

1 red
2 pink
3 yellow
4 green
5 blue
8 orange

Side End Section Stencil for Country Garden Shelf

Color Print for Country Garden Shelf

on the color print, paint one side of the design. Matching the flowers, flip the stencil at the side of the center section. Then paint the other side of the design.

When the small blue flowers are cut out, the little dotlike flower centers will also fall out. Simply paint the flowers, making the color darker at the edges. Then dip a small camel-hair watercolor brush into the stencil paint and place a dot of yellow in the center of each flower.

Flowers shown as pink, red, and orange on the drawings should be painted pink. (The color differentiation is merely to separate the overlays.) Then, as each layer is painted, apply just a touch of dark-rose color at the base. Shade the leaves with darker green in the same manner.

When the paint is dry, spray the entire shelf with one of the protective finishes.

Materials

Shelf about 34″ long, with an
    apron 4″ to 6″ deep
Paints
    White primer-sealer
    White base coat
    Stencil paints: pastel pink,
        blue, yellow, green, deep
        rose, dark green
Final finish: either gloss glaze
    coat or matte finish varnish

BLUE BOWS
PLACE MAT

Blue bows, pristine white batiste, and elegant Swiss eyelet edging make a place mat fine enough to be used with the most beautiful china, but one not so delicate that it can't be used for casual dining or even for a picnic in the park. For a Sunday concert on the spacious lawn of beautiful, historic Bullock Hall in Roswell, Georgia, the setting included blue-and-white china, crystal goblets, and even an old quilt. Cold chicken and potato salad never looked prettier!

INSTRUCTIONS

Review checklist (page 16) and assemble all basic stenciling supplies. Review the materials list for this project (page 38)

Wash and iron the white batiste. Work on a pulled thread or tear the fabric to make certain its edges are straight. Then cut two rectangles, each 13″ × 17½″. Following the drawing for the corner of the mat (page 38), on one piece measure 2⁵⁄₁₆″ from the corner along the horizontal and vertical straight edges, and make a mark at points A and B. Lay a straight edge on the line between these marks and draw the diagonal shown by the finely dotted line on the drawing. Repeat for all four cor-

ners. Cut on the lines you have just drawn.

Measure ½″ in from the cut edges of the mat and mark the seam line. Measure ½″ in from the seam line and draw the quilting line.

The bows on the place mat are the same as the bow on the Country Pinks Pillow (page 71). Trace that bow, then reduce it to 88 percent of the original.

Trace the side and top flower and ribbon sprays shown here. Using the Color Key, color the tracing and the reduced bow copy. Place the stencil film over the drawings and cut an overlay for each color. Remember that the two shades of blue on the bow indicate that there are to be two overlays, but both are to be painted with the same blue.

Mark the center top of the place mat and place it so that the top loops of the bow are ¼″ inside the quilting line and the bow is centered. Then stencil one blue bow. Move the stencils and paint one bow diagonally at each side, also ¼″ inside the quilting line. Place the flower sprays at top and sides as shown in the photograph. Lay the batiste over the drawings and, with the dark-green fabric marker, trace the flower stems, the veins in the leaves, and the flower-center accents of tiny green dots.

Set the color as recommended by the paint manufacturer. Place the back of the mat on a flat surface; lay the quilt batting over it, topping the batting with the stenciled top wrong side up. Pin together, carefully smoothing out all layers. Stitch all three layers together on the stitching line, leaving an opening about six inches across the bottom for turning. Trim all three layers, clipping corners

Blue Bows Place Mat

and trimming away the quilt batting in the seam allowance. Turn right side out. Stitch opening to close.

Trim the batiste edge from the Swiss eyelet close to the embroidery. Place the mat on a flat surface. Pin the eyelet in place, marking for darts to miter the corners. Remove the pins. Stitch the miters. Working from the right side, stitch the eyelet to the outside edge of the mat by hand or with a sewing machine, using a very tiny zigzag stitch.

Quilt on the marked line, either by hand or machine.

A pretty matching napkin edged with lace can be made with just a bit of the flower spray in the corner.

Materials (for one place mat)

Fabric and Sewing Supplies
  ½ yard white batiste, 45"
    wide
  1⅞ yards white Swiss eye-
    let, 1½" wide
  Quilt batting, 13" × 17½"
  White sewing thread
Stenciling Supplies
  Stencil paints: phthalo
    blue, grass green, pastel
    pink, bright yellow
  Dark-green fabric marker
    with fine point
Size: 12" × 16½" exclusive of
  1½" Swiss eyelet edging

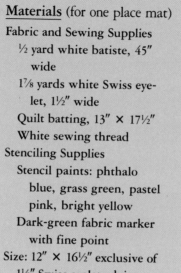

Side Spray

Color Key

2 pink
3 yellow
4 green
5 blue

cutting line

seam line

quilting line

2 5/16 "   B

2 5/16 "

Corner of the Mat

Top Spray

Top Spray Stencil for Blue Bows Place Mat

CANDLE BOX AND WALLPAPER BORDER WITH BRIGHT APPLES

Acandle box for keeping a ready supply of lights was a useful and practical piece of kitchen equipment in Colonial days. It was often decorated with a painted flower or stencil. Today's box can still hold candles, but is also handy for all kinds of other uses. This box is pine, finished with a natural color outside and a wonderful green and dark red inside. The apples, painted with a transparent japan paint that allows some of the wood grain to show, are bright and tempting. A slight antique effect has been added to give overall depth.

Notice the difference in appearance between the japanned apples on the box and those on the wallpaper border, which was worked with stencil crayons. Both are beautiful, just a bit different in feeling.

The color print shown here and the greeting card pictured in the candle box show the apples placed against the grid of a lattice pattern. This easy background, which is part of the Antiqued Tote design (page 132), adds a relaxed country texture. To achieve this look, first paint the apples, then place the lattice stencil, masking the openings where the grid would cover the apples. That lattice pattern can be very useful!

INSTRUCTIONS

Review checklist (page 16) and assemble all basic stenciling supplies. Review the materials list for this project.

If the wood is new, sand and clean. Apply several coats of the dark-green acrylic base coat

Color Print for Bright Apples with Lattice

Materials

Wood candle box or other open box, about 13″ × 5½″ × 4½″

Paints

  Acrylic base coats: forest green, bright red

  Stencil paints: japan paints in bright red, golden yellow, dark green, deep brown, black

Final finish: clear varnish, linseed oil, mineral spirits

  Small tube of burnt umber artist's oil paint

Candle Box and Wallpaper Border with Bright Apples

Stencil for Bright Apples

Color Key
1 red
3 yellow
4 green
8 orange
9 brown

Color Print for Bright Apples

to the inside of the box. Seal the natural wood of the outside of the box with clear varnish. Paint the edges of the box red as shown in the photograph on page 40.

Trace the apple stencil design, and color the drawing with the colors indicated by the numbers in the Color Key. Cut a stencil for each color. (The yellow and brown can be put on one stencil without a problem.) Using the dry-brush method and japan paints, stencil one copy of the design on each end of the box.

Center just one apple on the front of the box, using the elements of the design shown in the photograph. Place the full design on each side of the center apple. Dip a fine watercolor brush into a mixture of black and green, and paint the veins in the leaves. Dry the stencil paint overnight.

Mix equal portions of mineral spirits, linseed oil, and burnt umber pigment to make an antiquing solution. Apply to outside of box with a small sponge or brush. Rub down with a clean rag to remove most of the stain, leaving the color deeper at the edges and almost invisible at the center. Dry thoroughly. Finish inside and out with several coats of high-gloss varnish.

To copy the apple wall border shown in the photograph, using the design in the size given here, purchase white, prepasted wallpaper borders in the five-inch width. Paint with red, green, brown, and yellow stencil crayons or paints, spacing the apples at pleasing intervals. The border design may also be painted directly on a wall with the same colors and paints.

TISSUE BOX

This charming bathroom or desk accessory is one of those little touches that often mean much more than their size would indicate. Its design is adapted from a motif that might have been embroidered on an eighteenth-century crewel bedcover. Stenciled in pale pastels, the flowers look freshly picked.

This versatile pattern would adapt well as an overall design for walls, and it would also make a pretty border atop a chair rail or an interesting book cover or quilt square. Imagine a crib or doll quilt with the eighteenth-century border on the sashing and a different pastel flower stenciled in each square!

INSTRUCTIONS

Review checklist (page 16) and assemble all basic stenciling supplies. Review the materials list for this project.

Materials
Wood tissue box, approximately 5″ × 5″ × 6″
Paints
    White acrylic base coat
    Stencil crayons: medium green, pastel violet
Final finish: spray glaze coat

Color Print for Tissue Box

Floral Stencil for Sides of Tissue Box

Color Key
1 red
4 green

Eighteenth Century Border Stencil

If necessary, clean and sand to prepare box for painting. Apply three or four coats of white base coat as needed. Allow to dry.

Trace both the floral and the eighteenth-century border patterns. Following the Color Key, color the copies as suggested. Cut one stencil for the design elements colored red, and one for those colored green. (Paint the stencil colored red with the pastel violet paint; use the green paint, as expected, for the green stencil.)

Position the border pattern as shown in the photograph and paint it onto the top and bottom of all four sides of the box. In addition, paint the border around the four sides of the top of the box, mitering the corners to make a continuous border.

Place the floral spray in the center of the panel on each side of the box. Then paint, and dry the stenciling overnight. Spray with several light coats of glaze for a beautiful glossy finish.

Tissue Box

MEAGAN'S LITTLE CABINET

Although we purchased this piece new and unfinished, an antique or country "find" needing just a little paint also could be used to produce a special decorative accent. Seven-year-old Meagan loved the door and the shelf inside and she stenciled it herself for her own room, proving once again that stenciling is an art that children love and can practice with great success.

The cabinet is white with moldings in pastel pink, celadon green, and a pale-gold metallic compound called "White Fire." The green bows and pink flowers in the stencil designs echo the colors in the trim. The same ideas for painting could be used for any cabinet.

The flowers and wheat in the stencil design match those in the spray used for the Country Candle Sconce (page 139). The bow

Meagan's Little Cabinet

Bow and Floral Spray Color Print for Sides of Cabinet

Materials

Small wood cabinet, either
    new or a "found" piece
Paints
    White acrylic base coat
    Small jars of "folk-art"
        acrylic paints in celadon
        green and pastel pink
    Stencil paints: pastel pink,
        green, pale gold
    "White Fire" gold metallic
        compound
Final finish
    Spray glaze coat

Floral Stencil for Cabinet Door

Color Key

1 red
2 pink
3 yellow
4 green
7 light green

and the floral spray stencils are shown separately (page 49 for greater flexibility. Use the color print as a guide in placing the spray with the bow.

INSTRUCTIONS

Review checklist (page 16) and assemble all basic stenciling supplies. Review the materials list for this project (page 47).

Clean and/or sand, and take care of any other prepainting needs; then paint the cabinet with several coats of white base coat. Paint the moldings in pink, green, and metallic gold, as shown in the photograph. Highlight any details, such as the grooves on the door and sides, with gold accents.

Trace the design for the door. On another piece of paper, trace the bow for the sides of the cabinet. Place the drawing of the bow over the flower spray and, using the color print as a guide for placement, trace the flower spray. Using the Color Key, color the tracing as indicated by the numbers. Cut a stencil for each color. Substitute green for blue for the bow and follow the color print as you paint the bow and flower design on each side of the cabinet.

Placing it as shown in the photograph and using the same colors, paint the spray on the door. Dry thoroughly. If a high gloss is desired, use spray glaze. Substitute matte finish if you prefer. The final spray adds protection for the metallic paint and retards tarnish.

Bow Stencil

Floral Stencil for Cabinet Sides

49

TULIP FLOWER POTS

Ordinary clay pots can be transformed into attractive "porcelain" containers through the magic of paint. Several coats of stain-killing primer are used to cover the clay, and flat white latex enamel forms a base for a sponged background and a stencil pattern. A thick coat of spray glaze protects all and adds a deep shine.

Though it is not recommended that you plant directly in these pots, a live plant in another container, sitting on a plastic saucer to protect the paint from moisture, will do well in these country vessels. Two tulip designs—one for textured sponging, one for a plain background—offer a choice of styles, and two borders enhance the rim of the pots.

NOTE: Clay pots vary greatly in dimension. A six-inch pot will probably be 6″ across the top, but its height might range from 4″ to 7″, depending upon the manufacturer. The individual tulip motifs of this design will fit most pots since they are applied separately and the spacing can easily be adjusted. For much larger pots, the tulips may be enlarged by using a copier (see page 18).

INSTRUCTIONS

Review checklist (page 16) and assemble all basic stenciling supplies. Review the materials list for this project (page 53).

Wash pots to remove any dust or oil. Dry well, at least overnight. (Clay pots absorb water and feel dry even though moisture is trapped inside.) Paint the pots with two coats of white stain-killing primer. (The first coat will dry almost immediately because the clay absorbs all moisture.)

Add two coats of flat white latex. Dry thoroughly.

Blue Pot. Pour a small amount of light-blue stencil paint into a small, flat saucer. Pour a similar amount of the medium-blue paint directly onto the light blue. Follow with like amounts of extender and thickener poured onto the two paints. Slant and rotate the saucer to mix slightly.

Dampen a small sponge in water and wring out well. Dip the sponge lightly into the paint mixture. Dab the sponge on a clean piece of absorbent paper and practice the pattern you wish to use. Best results are obtained

Chunky Tulip Flower Pots with Blue Sponging

Classic Tulip Flower Pot

when the sponge is almost dry and the paint is applied sparingly. Try to achieve a random pattern, allowing the white background to be more important than the color. When you are satisfied with the test pattern on the paper, apply the sponge pattern to the pot. Dry.

Trace the Chunky Tulip design and color the tracing with the two shades of blue indicated by numbers 5 and 6 in the color key. Cut a stencil for each shade of blue.

Apply the Chunky Tulip design with the medium-blue paint, spacing the motifs evenly around the pot: On the pots shown in the photographs there are four tulips with about ½" space between the ends of the leaves at the tops.

Use the ribbon beading border (page 29) for the rim of the pot, and paint it with the same blue as was used for the tulips. Dry.

White Pot. Paint the pot white as de-scribed above. Trace the Classic Tulip design. Color the tracing red, yellow, and green, following the numbers in the **Color Key.** Cut one stencil for each color.

Using the red, green, and yellow stencil paints, stencil the tulips around the base of the pot. On this 8" pot there are six tulips with about ¾" space between the tips of the leaves. Use the tulip border on the upper rim of the pot.

Trace the scalloped border (#12 on page 29) and cut a stencil. Using green paint, stencil the border around the lower edge of the pot as illustrated in the photograph.

Both Pots. Spray with several coats of spray glaze, coating the inside of the pot as well as the outside to protect against moisture. Find a pretty plant, and enjoy an inexpensive country accent on the porch or in the sun room.

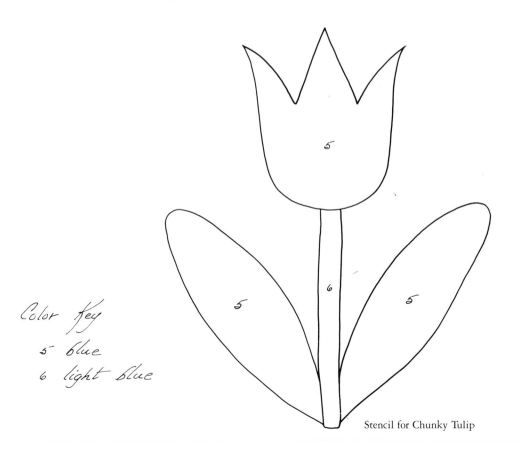

Color Key
5 blue
6 light blue

Stencil for Chunky Tulip

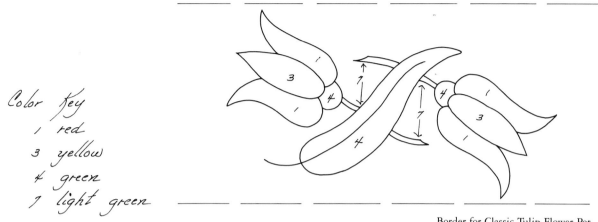

Color Key
1 red
3 yellow
4 green
7 light green

Border for Classic Tulip Flower Pot

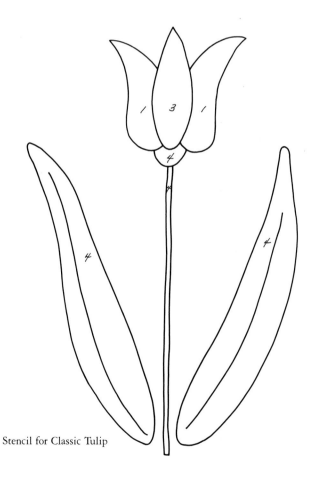

Stencil for Classic Tulip

Materials

Clay pots: the ones shown in the photograph are 6″ and 8″

Paints

    Flat white latex base coat

    White alcohol-based, stain-killing primer

    Stencil paints:

        Blue pots: medium blue, pale blue

        White pot: bright red, grass green, primary yellow

Small marine or cellulose sponge for the blue pots

Extender and thickener for the blue pots

Final finish: spray glaze coat

HEART-SHAPED SHELF

S weetly painted, this little shelf is a pretty addition to a little girl's room. By staining the wood with a natural finish instead of using glossy white enamel, the same shelf can be used in a country hallway or entrance. The heart-shaped flowers on this useful shelf and peg hook echo the shape of the shelf itself.

INSTRUCTIONS

Review checklist (page 16) and assemble all basic stenciling supplies. Review the materials list for this project.

Trace the two sprays of heart-shaped flowers. Color the tracings as indicated in the Color Key and cut one stencil for pink, one for green. Trace the narrow heart border (#2, page 28). Cut one pink and one green stencil.

After the shelf has been sanded and prepared for painting, apply a coat of white primer-sealer and several coats of white base-coat paint. Paint the outside edge of the heart with green stencil paint. Paint the grooved edges of the heart and the shelf with the pink stencil paint, as shown in the photograph. Dry.

Place the sprays of flowers, the leaves, and the border as shown in the photograph, and paint. If there is sufficient space on your shelf, use the lower outside leaf of the spray with three flowers to apply a single leaf on each side of the underside of the shelf. Dry. Spray with glaze coat to simulate a high-gloss enamel.

Heart-Shaped Shelf

Right Spray Stencil for Heart-Shaped Shelf

Materials

Small heart-shaped shelf,
   about 12″ at widest point
Paints
   White primer-sealer
   White acrylic base coat
   Stencil paints: pastel pink,
      medium green
Final finish: spray glaze coat

Left Spray Stencil for Heart-Shaped Shelf

QUILTED BRIDAL WREATH PILLOW

Through the magic of stenciling you can create in minutes a fabric design for a pillow that, if appliquéd, would take weeks of careful sewing. The antique appearance afforded by stenciling is easy to duplicate and very quickly creates a look of country elegance. An experienced quilter will appreciate how much easier it is to paint intricate leaves and stems than to cut and stitch them. Quilting the pillow adds wonderful dimension to the stenciled design.

INSTRUCTIONS

Review checklist (page 16) and assemble all basic stenciling supplies. Review the materials list for this project (page 58).

Wash the fabric to remove sizing and iron well. Cut two 12″ squares of muslin, one to stencil, the other to use as backing for the quilting fleece or batting. Fold one square into quarters, and press to mark the lines thus made.

Trace or copy the stencil design and color, following the numbers in the **Color Key**. Cut a stencil for each color. (Since they are so far apart, it will be both convenient and thrifty to cut both the yellow and green on the same overlay.)

The stencil shows the center flower and two of the four flowers which will surround it in the completed design. The flower at the upper left, which is not connected to another with a curved stem, is the center flower. Place this flower over the center point of the fabric. The two small arrows should fall on the pressed fold-lines of the muslin.

Stencil the three flowers with rose fabric paint or stencil crayon, shading the color from dark at the edges to nothing in the centers. If you prefer a deeper pink that extends to the yellow centers, save the flower centers when you cut them and hold them in place while stenciling the pink flowers. This will protect the fabric underneath and ensure that the yellow will be pure when painted.

Paint the leaves and stem green, keeping the color slightly uneven for an aged look.

Rotate the stencil, matching the center flower and one other by way of using them as registration marks. Repeat the color steps until the design is completed. Set the color as recommended by the paint manufacturer.

Layer together the stenciled muslin, the quilting fleece or batting, and the plain muslin square. Pin together and baste securely.

Quilt around all the stenciled areas. If desired, a second row of stitches may be placed inside the flowers, following the scalloped outline. For a beautiful addition, you can quilt the background area outside the flower wreath in a tiny diamond pattern. To place these lines, use ½″ masking tape and stitch along the edge of the tape.

To construct the pillow, cut from the printed fabric a 12″ square for backing. Make a double-layered ruffle, cutting one ruffle 3½″ wide, the other 2¾″ wide. Each ruffle should be at least 120″ long to gather correctly. Finish

Quilted Bridal Wreath Pillow

the ruffle with a narrow hem and narrow lace edging if desired. Layer the two ruffles together and gather as one, pulling up fullness to fit outside edge of pillow.

Trim the edges of the quilted top to 12″.

Join the top, backing, and the ruffle in a seam and stitch, leaving an opening for turning. Trim seam and corners. Turn right side out and stuff with fiberfill. Stitch opening closed.

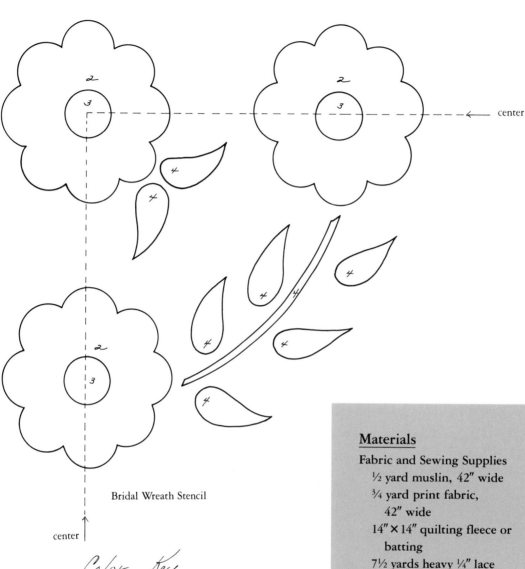

center ←

Bridal Wreath Stencil

center ↑

Color Key
2 pink
3 yellow
4 green

Materials
Fabric and Sewing Supplies
½ yard muslin, 42″ wide
¾ yard print fabric,
  42″ wide
14″ × 14″ quilting fleece or
  batting
7½ yards heavy ¼″ lace
  edging
Quilting thread
Quilting needle
Fiberfill to stuff pillow
Masking tape, ½″ wide
Stenciling Supplies
Fabric paints or stencil
  crayons: rose, green,
  gold

Size: 11″ × 11″, plus 3″ ruffle

ROSE OF SHARON QUILT

Among the most treasured and sought-after collectibles today, crib and doll quilts are wonderful projects for today's busy world. Small quilts, which do not need a bulky quilting frame, require less work and are thus easy to finish quickly.

A traditional appliqué quilt pattern adapted to stenciling makes a lovely small cover to be used as a lap robe or baby blanket. The colors in this quilt are very pale pastels, perfect for the latter. The use of a low-loft batting produces a less bulky quilt, making the tiny stitches of yesteryear possible once again. To suggest the delicate softness of an old quilt, the fabric used here is a finely woven all-cotton batiste of the same quality that might be used for a baby dress.

Size: 35″ × 45″. Although this quilt has been miniaturized for use as a crib cover or lap throw, it may be made larger by adding

Color Print for Rose of Sharon

This print was made in blue to show the effect of a different color choice.

squares or enlarging the squares. In most old quilts of this pattern, the white squares measure approximately 12″ rather than 8″, as shown here. To enlarge the design motif to fit a 12″ square, trace the pattern, then use a copy machine to increase the size to 150 percent of the original.

Note: The yardages for fabric include ¼ yard extra to allow for shrinkage and for cutting on a pulled thread or tearing to straighten the edges, if this has not been done.

INSTRUCTIONS

Review checklist (page 16) and assemble all basic stenciling supplies. Review the materials list for this project.

Wash both the pink and the white batiste to remove the sizing. Press. Pulling threads to mark cutting lines, cut 12 white 9″ × 9″ squares.

Trace the Rose of Sharon pattern and, following the Color Key, color the tracing to match the numbers on the pattern. Cut three stencils: one for the portion of the rose shown as pink, one for the red portion, and one for placing both the yellow and green elements on one stencil.

Centering the design on a white square, begin with the stencil for the pink areas. Apply the pink paint more heavily around the edges of the stencil, feathering and blending it so the center of the flower remains white.

Next, place the stencil for red, centering the cut-out area over the pink just painted. It will extend over some of the pink just applied. Use the same pink paint as for the first overlay. The overlapping of color will create a deeper tone. Again, feather the color to leave the center area white.

Position the green and yellow stencil. Paint the flower center yellow, shading it darker at the edges. Finish by painting the leaves. (On many of the traditional appliquéd Rose of Sharon quilts, the outside portion of the flower and the center are cut from pale pink and the inner section of the flower from a deeper shade of pink, rather than using yellow for the center, as shown here. This alternate coloring is possible with this method of stenciling. Try a sample to see which you prefer.)

Stencil the Rose of Sharon on all 12 white squares, keeping the intensity of coloring as nearly alike as possible. Set the color as recommended by the paint manufacturer.

Materials
Fabric and Sewing Supplies
 1½ yards white 100 percent cotton batiste or muslin, 45″ wide
 2½ yards pale-pink 100 percent cotton batiste or muslin
 Low-loft quilt batting, at least 36″ × 45″
 White quilting thread
 #10 between quilting needle
Stenciling Supplies
 Stencil paints or fabric dyes: pastel pink, pale green, pastel yellow

Rose of Sharon Quilt

Tear the pink fabric for sashing. You will need eight strips 9″ × 3″, three strips 30″ × 3″, two strips 4″ × 30″, and two strips 50″ × 4″. Tear the two 50″ strips vertically along the selvage and the other pieces across the fabric.

Making ½″ seams throughout, using white sewing thread, and beginning with the short sashing strips, assemble three white squares and two pink strips into a 29″ piece. Make four such pieces. Press the seams toward the pink. Join the four long pieces with the three 30″ sashing strips, again pressing the seams toward the pink. Be certain to tear the strips so that a piece 36″ × 46″ will remain for the quilt back.

Sew a 4″ strip to the top and bottom of the piece. Trim the extra length of the pink so that it is even with the white. Press seam toward the pink as before. The pieced top should measure 36″ × 46″.

Press both the pieced quilt top and the pink quilt back. Lay the back flat and place the quilt batting on top. Then place the sten-ciled piece—design side up—on top. Match edges and pin the layers together securely. Using long stitches, baste the three layers together.

Stitching with white quilting thread, quilt around all elements of the stenciled designs, along the colored edges. Also quilt around the inside of each white block, placing the stitching ¼″ inside the stitching lines.

When all quilting is complete, baste the raw outside edges together, placing the stitches about ½″ from the cut edges. Trim the edges evenly.

Cut enough 1½″ bias strips from the remaining white batiste to reach around the outside edges of the quilt (about 4½ yards). Seam to make a continuous piece.

With right sides together, stitch the binding to the right side of the quilt, allowing enough extra fullness at the four corners to make a neat mitered turn. Press the binding to the wrong side of the quilt, fold under ½″ and, with invisible stitches, fasten the binding to the wrong side of the quilt.

Stencil for Rose of Sharon

Color Key
1 red
2 pink
3 yellow
4 green

DOLL CRADLE

Pink and green sponging, green bows, and little pink hearts trim a doll cradle that any little girl would love. If her bedroom is decorated in country style, this cradle will be a delightful addition. Sturdy and large enough to hold a good-sized doll, it will be prized for many years to come.

The sponging technique provides an attractive painted finish that adds texture and a country air. The pink and green that have been sponged onto the ivory background are echoed in the stenciled bows and hearts. For a very special addition, consider using the bow and hearts to make a stenciled doll quilt and pillow to match the cradle.

INSTRUCTIONS

Review checklist (page 16) and assemble all basic stenciling supplies. Review the materials list for this project.

If necessary, sand the cradle to prepare for painting. Apply two or three coats of off-white base coat, rubbing lightly with steel wool between applications. Paint the edges of the end panels and the rockers pale green.

In a small, shallow saucer, pour a small amount of the green stencil paint in a circular pattern. Swirl pink on top. Follow with thickener and extender. Tilt and rotate the saucer to stir the liquids slightly.

Wet a sponge in water and wring it out well. Dip the sponge into the paint mixture.

Practice making a sponging pattern on paper. Notice that the patterns become prettier as the sponge becomes dry. This is the point at which to begin sponging the cradle. Apply the sponge pattern to the outside of the cradle.

Trace the pattern for the Country Bow and cut a stencil for it. Position it as shown in the color photograph and paint it green.

Trace the three hearts and cut a stencil for each. Place the heart stencils randomly on the end and side panels of the cradle and paint them pink. Dry. Spray with several coats of glaze.

Materials

Unfinished wood doll cradle, about 18″ long
Paints
  Acrylic base coats: off-white, pale green
  Stencil paints: pastel pink, pastel green
  Extender
  Thickener
Final finish: spray glaze coat

Doll Cradle

Hearts and Bow Stencil for Doll Cradle

COUNTRY PINKS

COUNTRY PINKS PILLOW

The sprightly Country Pink, fragrant and graceful, lends its charm to this group of three pillows. When bluebirds and blue ribbons are added and the pillows are finished with heirloom details and lace, the series becomes very special indeed. A wall border stenciled on prepasted paper adds a finishing touch. Country and the joy of springtime have easily become part of your room!

Color Print for Country Pinks

68

Country Pinks Pillow, Country Pinks Wallpaper Border, Pinks on the
Diagonal Pillow, and Bluebirds and Blue Ribbons Pillow

INSTRUCTIONS

Review checklist (page 16) and assemble all basic stenciling supplies. Review the materials list for this project.

Trace the design, and cut one stencil for each color shown on the drawing.

Wash the batiste to remove the sizing. Iron well. Cut two 12″ squares of fabric, one for the front and one for the back of the pillow. Working across the full width of the remaining batiste, cut two ruffle strips 3″ wide.

Using the tracing of the full stencil pattern, decide upon the placement of the design. Stencil the bow first, using the same blue for both stencils. Next stencil the green, then the pink portions of the design. Study the color print for this design and note how the flowers are shaded. The entire flower was painted pale pink. Then a small amount of rose was added at the base of the flower and rubbed into the pink to produce deep shading at the base of the flower which blends into the pink at the tips of the petals. This same method was used for the color green: A small amount of blue was placed in the center portion of the leaves and then blended into the green.

Place the tracing of the full stencil pattern under the stenciled pillow top. With the fabric marker, add the flower stems and the veins in the leaves as illustrated in the color print.

To set the color, follow the manufacturer's instructions on the paint package.

Make the piping with the balance of the batiste and the cotton cording. Join the ruffle strips into a single piece and attach the lace edging. Make three tiny pin tucks parallel to the lace edging. Gather the ruffle. Pin piping and ruffle to the front of the pillow. Leaving an opening at the bottom of the pillow for stuffing, join pillow front to back in a seam which encloses the ruffle and piping. Turn right side out. Fill evenly with fiberfill. Sew opening to close.

Materials

Fabric and Sewing Supplies
¾ yard pale-cream batiste, 45″ wide
2½ yards cream-color cotton lace edging, 1″ wide
1¼ yards cotton cording
Fiberfill to stuff pillow
Pale-cream sewing thread
Stenciling Supplies
Stencil paints: phthalo blue, grass green, pink, rose
Dark-green fabric marker with fine point

Size: 11″ × 11″, plus 3″ ruffle

Country Pinks Pillow Stencil, traced
and colored with pencils.

BLUEBIRDS AND BLUE RIBBONS PILLOW

INSTRUCTIONS

Review checklist (page 16) and assemble all basic stenciling supplies. Review the materials list for this project (page 74).

Wash the batiste to remove the sizing, then iron. Cut two pieces measuring 10½″ × 17″ for the pillow front and back. (Seam allowance is ½″.)

On tracing paper, draw a rectangle 10½″ × 17″. Mark the center of the rectangle. Trace the bow from the Country Pinks Pillow on page 71, placing the knot of the bow on the marked center of the rectangle.

Place the tracing of the bow over the bluebird drawing and trace the bluebird, flower, and streamers to the right of the bow, keeping the bird's full front wing tip one inch from the top line of the rectangle. The pointed end of the trailing ribbon which flows to the left should join the knot of the bow. This position will place the void (see drawing) just after the section of ribbon under the loop of the bow. Check your placement against the reduced color print.

Fold the tracing in half vertically. Trace the bird, streamers, flower, and the ribbon connected to the bow just as far as the loop of the bow. Trace the tip of the ribbon inside the loop. Then draw freehand a short piece of ribbon to fill in the short gap shown in the drawing.

Following the numbers from the Color Keys of the two drawings, color the completed drawing. To avoid cutting a complete stencil for each color, cut stencils as follows: one for light blue, pink, and yellow; one for blue and green. Use the same blue for painting both the blue and the light-blue sections of the design. Two shades have been used merely to divide the stencil overlays.

When painting the bluebirds, note how the birds have been shaded. To shade the wings and tail, make the color heavier along the edges. Leave the breast area unpainted, then gently shade the area with rose. Make the flowers solid pink, then add a touch of rose at the base of the flowers and shade it into the pink.

Place the completed piece over the stencil pattern on the book page and, with the dark-green fabric marker, trace in the flower, stems, and leaves. Use the black pen for the bird eyes. (If your fabric marker is new or likely to bleed through the fabric and stain the page, place a piece of tracing paper between the fabric and the page.)

Set the color according to the paint manufacturer's instructions.

From the batiste fabric, cut across the full width of the fabric to make three ruffle strips 6″ wide. Join the seams to make a continuous piece. Fold in half to make a 3″-wide double ruffle. The ruffle on the pillow in the photograph has been finished with a tiny machine-made scallop. Stitched with thread

Bluebirds and Blue Ribbons Pillow

matching the batiste, this is an elegant final touch. Gather the raw edge of the ruffle to fit the pillow top.

From the remaining batiste, cut a bias strip 1″ wide to cover the cording. Pin the covered cording to the pillow top, then pin the gathered ruffle to the top. Place the back of the pillow on the top, matching edges. Pin, then seam, leaving a 6″ opening at the bottom of the pillow for stuffing. Trim the corners and seam where necessary. Turn right side out. Stuff with fiberfill. Stitch the opening closed with invisible stitches.

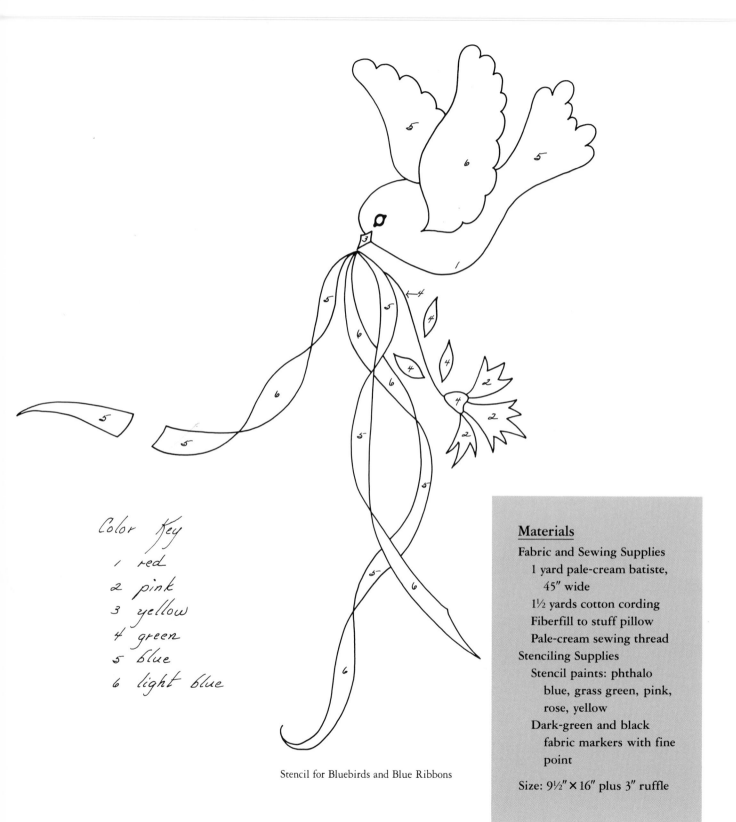

Color Key

1 red
2 pink
3 yellow
4 green
5 blue
6 light blue

Stencil for Bluebirds and Blue Ribbons

Materials

Fabric and Sewing Supplies
  1 yard pale-cream batiste,
    45" wide
  1½ yards cotton cording
  Fiberfill to stuff pillow
  Pale-cream sewing thread
Stenciling Supplies
  Stencil paints: phthalo
    blue, grass green, pink,
    rose, yellow
  Dark-green and black
    fabric markers with fine
    point

Size: 9½" × 16" plus 3" ruffle

Color Print for Bluebirds and Blue Ribbons

PINKS ON THE DIAGONAL PILLOW AND WALLPAPER BORDER

INSTRUCTIONS

    Review checklist (page 16) and assemble all basic stenciling supplies. Review the materials list for this project.

    Trace the Pinks border pattern; color the pink and green elements as suggested. Cut one stencil for the rose and one for the green portions of the design. On the green stencil, cut a very fine line for the flower stems as indicated on the stencil pattern.

    Wash the batiste to remove the sizing. Iron well. Cut two 12" squares, one for the front and one for the back of the pillow. Cut two 12" squares of quilting fleece.

Materials for Pillow

Fabric and Sewing Supplies
  ½ yard pale-cream batiste, 45" wide
  2¼ yards Swiss eyelet edging, 4" wide
  1¼ yards cotton cording
  Fiberfill to stuff pillow
  ½ yard quilting fleece
  Pale-cream sewing thread

Stenciling Supplies
  Stencil paints: grass green, rose
  Dark-green fabric marker with the fine point
  Blue washout pen for marking fabric

Color Print for Pinks on the Diagonal

Pinks on the Diagonal Pillow and Wallpaper Border

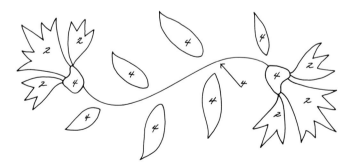

Color Key

2 pink
4 green

Stencil for Pinks on the Diagonal

Fold one of the batiste squares diagonally from corner to corner to establish the first diagonal line as shown on the Guide for Marking Diagonals (below). Measure 1¾" out from that line and, with the blue washout pen, draw a second diagonal line. Continue marking diagonals at 1¾" intervals until the entire square is marked as shown on the Guide. When marking with the washout pen, make the lines as light as possible.

Starting with the stripes on either side of the center line marked a/b on the Guide and spacing the pink motifs about ½" apart, paint the pinks between the lines. Remember that there is a ½" seam allowance. A small portion of design may extend into the seam allowance in some stripes, but this only adds to the beauty of the piece.

Place the stenciled piece over the original design and, with the dark-green pen, draw the veins in the leaves. Set the color following the manufacturer's instructions on the paint package.

Place a square of quilting fleece on the back of the stenciled fabric. Pin the two together and quilt by stitching on the blue lines by hand or machine. Sponge off the blue markings.

To make self-piping, cover the cording with bias strips cut from the remaining batiste.

Join the Swiss eyelet edging with a tiny seam. Gather the raw edge and pull up the gathers to fit the pillow top. Pin the cording to the painted pillow top, matching the raw edges and clipping at the corners. Stitch. Pin the gathered ruffle to the top, right sides together.

To make a prettier pillow by giving the back of the pillow the same weight as the front, pin the pillow back and quilting fleece together. Treating the two layers as one, stitch them to the pillow front, leaving a 5" opening at the bottom for stuffing. Trim corners and seam if necessary. Turn right side out. Fill with fiberfill. Close opening with invisible stitches.

This strippable wallpaper border was prepasted and with the blue stripes already printed. It is available in both four- and seven-inch widths in either white or ivory, and either plain or with blue or rose borders. This is a very practical purchase, since it is certainly easier to paint a border sitting at a desk than hanging over a step ladder. Though this paper border is usually found in crafts stores, there may be adaptable papers in wallpaper stores.

To make this border, enlarge the Pinks border to 185 percent and paint it with the same colors used for the pillow. Many of the designs in this book can be adapted for this kind of alternate application. The apples (page 41) and pineapple (page 83) are two examples, but there are many other possibilities as well.

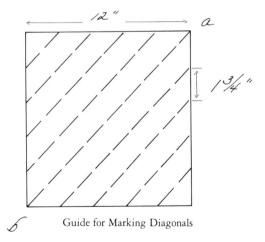

Guide for Marking Diagonals

COUNTRY PINEAPPLES

COUNTRY PINEAPPLE WALL BORDER

Though it looks like a large project, the wall border is easily manageable, particularly if worked in either water-based stencil paints or with stencil crayons, both of which allow for quick cleanup. By working in small time allotments, you'll find the job is soon finished!

INSTRUCTIONS

Review checklist (page 16) and assemble all basic stenciling supplies. Review the materials list for this project (page 82).

After tracing the pineapple on page 83, color the tracing using the numbers and **Color Key.** Cut four stencils: one for the pineapple scales (the yellow portions), one for each of the

T
he pineapple, traditional symbol of hospitality, makes a wonderful border placed on a buff-colored wall over a dark-green faux marble chair rail. Dark-green wallpaper under the chair rail adds a country look to the scheme.

Country Pineapple Wall Border, Country Pineapple Pillow, Little Pineapples Trinket Box, and Welcome Sign

Color Print for Country Pineapple

two shades of green, and one for the leaves shown as blue.

The photograph shows the stenciled pineapple border with the lower leaves positioned just above a green faux marble chair rail, with the pineapples placed so that there are eight inches between the center of one pineapple and the center of the next. However, you may prefer different spacing, and these pineapples may be placed closer or farther apart as needed. Also, the size of the pineapples may be enlarged or reduced by copy machine should another size be more appropriate for your needs.

You can fashion another wall border by using a section of the Country Gingham checks (page 84) between the pineapples as a spacer, as was done on the Quilted Pineapple Pillow. The color of the checks could match either the pineapple or the chair rail. Use the gingham squares in the size shown (page 84).

To achieve subtle variations of color, the following order was used in applying the stencil paints:

Pineapple: Follow an even coat of yellow overall, with a coat of yellow ocher applied heavier at the sides and bottom of the pineapple. Finally, add a very slight touch of burnt sienna at the bottom and sides, and blend softly into the ocher.

Leaves: Begin with a coat of yellow, followed by the medium green overall. Add phthalo green, blending it almost to the tips of the leaves. Put just a touch of phthalo blue at the base of the leaf and lightly carry it into the green to emphasize the base of the leaves. Use the same procedure for each successive overlay of leaf stencils, including those shown as blue on your tracing.

Add the veins in the leaves with the permanent marker.

Materials

Stencil paints: yellow ocher, burnt sienna, sunflower yellow, medium green, phthalo green, phthalo blue

Dark-green permanent marker with fine point

Color Key
3 yellow
4 green
5 blue
7 light green

Stencil for Country Pineapple

QUILTED PINEAPPLE PILLOW

I t is very satisfying to decorate a room by using matching motifs for both walls and fabric details. This plump pillow achieves that special touch quickly and easily by echoing the colors and design of the wall border. Note the couture feature of fine sewing in the double ruffle and the dainty green scalloped edging on those ruffles.

INSTRUCTIONS

Review checklist (page 16) and assemble all basic stenciling supplies. Review the materials list for this project.

Trace the pineapple on page 83. Enlarge it to 129 percent by copier. Color the tracing and cut four stencils as for the wall border.

Using a sheet of squared graph paper at least 15″ × 15″, trace the Country Gingham pattern (below), centering it on one side edge and repeating it to fill a length of 12″. Fold the paper or turn the pattern, and trace the other three sides to match. The enlarged pineapple should measure about 10¾″ and should be centered on the border so the leaves overlap into the border checks at top and bottom (see photograph).

Note that where the leaves extend into the gingham border, the shape of the checks will be changed accordingly. Cut one stencil for the top border, one for the bottom, and one for the sides.

From the fabric, cut three 14″ × 14″ squares. Wash to remove sizing and iron well. Stencil one square following the painting procedure for the wall border and painting the checks in the manner used for the pineapple scales. Add the veins in the leaves with the fabric marker.

Allow the paint to dry or set it as instructed by the manufacturer. Place the painted square, the quilt batting, and one

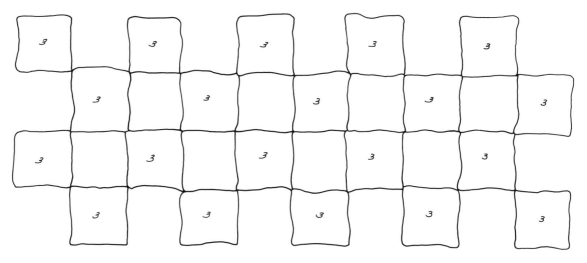

Country Gingham Stencil

Quilted Pineapple Pillow, upper right

plain square together in layers, with the quilt batting in the middle. Pin securely and baste together. Finally, outline quilt on all painted lines.

Trim the edges evenly so that the square measures 13″ × 13″. Make the ruffle from three 6″ strips of fabric joined into a single piece and folded in half horizontally to make a 3″ double ruffle. The pretty green edging on the pillow in the photograph was made by using green thread and a scallop stitch on the sewing machine. Stitch the scallop on the folded edge. Gather the raw edges to fit the pillow top.

Pin the gathered ruffle to the pillow top, and place the last square of fabric on top for a backing. Stitch the layers together in a ½″ seam, leaving an opening for stuffing. Trim the corners and turn right side out. Fill the pillow with fiberfill. Close opening.

Materials
Fabric and Sewing Supplies
1 yard off-white or ecru batiste or unbleached muslin, 45″ wide
15″ × 15″ low-loft quilt batting
Off-white or ecru quilting thread
Off-white or ecru sewing thread
Dark-green sewing thread for scalloped edge on ruffle
Fiberfill to stuff pillow
Dark-green permanent fabric marker
Paints as listed for wall border

Size: 12½″ × 12½″, plus 3″ ruffle

LITTLE PINEAPPLES TRINKET BOX

corners cut to suggest a hexagonal shape, a perfectly rectangular box will also be pretty adorned with these little pineapples. The size of the pineapples also can vary. You can enlarge the basic pineapple pattern by copier, or you can extend the corner motifs.

Cut one stencil for the entire design. The curving lines connecting the corner motifs may be cut as a fine line, or they may be added with the fine marker. Use pattern B for the box top and A for the front and back sides. For the end panels, use only one of the pineapples from pattern A, turning the pineapple so that it stands upright. Note that

INSTRUCTIONS

Review checklist (page 16) and assemble all basic stenciling supplies. Review the materials list for this project (page 89).

Although the box shown in the photograph is a very attractive one with its

Little Pineapples Trinket Box

A

Stencil for Little Pineapples

Color Print for Little Pineapples

B

Stencil for Little Pineapples Box Lid

on these tiny designs the bridges are very small, which makes the stencils quite fragile. Careful cutting and handling is all that is required to avoid problems.

Sand the box, and seal with a coat of clear varnish. When dry, place the stencils as shown in the photograph and paint with black. Add the veins in the leaves with the fine-point marker.

Mask the edges of the top of the box, and paint a ¼" gold leaf border. (See page 22 for instructions for mixing gold leaf powder.) Allow the gold leaf to dry overnight.

Make an antiquing solution by mixing equal parts of the clear varnish and the burnt umber artist's oil paint. Cover the entire box with the antiquing solution, avoiding the gold leaf as much as possible. When the antiquing is tacky, rub off the surplus, highlighting the center portions of the panels. Rub off any antiquing that has spread onto the gold leaf.

Finish with several coats of clear varnish.

Color Print for Little Pineapples Box Lid

WELCOME SIGN

The board pictured in the photograph has the familiar, inviting shape of an antique tavern sign. Gold leaf edges and the traditional pineapple to symbolize hospitality are accented by very slight ocher antiquing on the edges of the board.

This design would also be very attractive with a very dark-green, blue, or black background. Leave the pineapple as shown in the photograph and paint WELCOME with metallic gold or an antique shade of red.

INSTRUCTIONS

Review checklist (page 16) and assemble all basic stenciling supplies. Review the materials list for this project.

Sand and prepare the wood if it is new, and spray lightly with the acrylic sealer.

Mix extender with yellow ocher base coat in about a 50-50 solution. With a small sponge applicator, apply the mixture heavily around the edges of the board and very sparingly in the center. Allow to sit for a minute or two. While the mixture is still tacky and wet, wipe off the excess antiquing, using a clean, soft rag and working out from the middle of the plaque. Leave a heavier coat around the edges and highlight the middle.

Trace the large pineapple on page 83 and cut one stencil overlay for each color on the drawing (two green, one blue, one yellow ocher). Then trace and cut a stencil for the word WELCOME.

Place the curved lettering at the top of the sign, centering it and making certain the spacing of letters is correct in relation to the pineapple (see photograph). Paint the letters with the burnt sienna.

Materials

Wood sign board, approximately 10″ × 16″
Paints
   Acrylic sealer
   Extender
   Metallic gold-paste leafing compound
   Stencil paints: leaf green, yellow ocher, burnt sienna
Black permanent marker with fine point
Final finish: spray glaze coat

Welcome Sign

Stencil for Welcome Sign

Use this stencil with Country Pineapple (page 83) to create Welcome Sign.

Using yellow ocher, paint the pineapple. Then apply over the yellow ocher a very small amount of burnt sienna at the base and sides of the pineapple to add a delicate shading.

Using the green overlays, paint the leaves, applying the paint more heavily at the bases. Paint all leaves, including those shown as blue on the drawing, with the same leaf green paint.

When the paint is thoroughly dry, use the fine-point marker to add veins in the leaves and outline all areas of the design. Some of the color prints of other designs in this book use this technique. Examine one of them and notice that the lines are broken to add the appearance of age to the new paint. Using this kind of outlining on the sign makes the design motif stand out much clearer and brighter against the background.

Finally, paint the edges of the board with the gold metallic compound. Allow sufficient time for drying. Spray with glaze coat to protect the colors. If you prefer, a matte spray will also furnish protection and will make the sign look aged.

CLASSIC COUNTRY ELEGANCE

COUNTRY QUEEN ANNE TABLE

This little table with its distressed black paint, scalloped apron, lovely tapered legs, and pad feet could well be one of those pieces. The gold metallic stencil design with classic lines adds a special touch.

Although the table pictured in the photograph is new, the same ideas can be used to refinish an old table as well. The size of the stencil can be altered by copier to fit a table of another size or, alternatively, a box. Slightly enlarged, this design also can be used as a very classic border along a ceiling.

INSTRUCTIONS

Review checklist (page 16) and assemble all basic stenciling supplies. Review the materials list for this project.

S ome of the most desirable furniture collectibles are handmade pieces copied from fine antique collections. The craftsmen used whatever wood was on hand—usually pine—copied the basic lines, and added embellishments of their own.

End Section of Bow Stencil

> **Materials**
> Table, box, or wall for
>   stenciling
> Gold metallic compound
> Matte-finish sealer

Country Queen Anne Table

Trace the stencil design, joining the two sections by overlapping the leaves at the long broken line. Trace also the little bell flower design for the legs. Since this is a one-color design, it is necessary to cut only one stencil for each motif. On long stencils such as the bow and wreath, it is advisable to use spray adhesive to help hold the film in place. Although this will involve either cleaning the stencil or cutting a second half design, in the end this procedure will save time.

If you are working on a table, paint the design on the front and back aprons. Place the bell flower on the legs as shown in the photograph, and on the front, back, and sides. Apply the gold metallic compound with a light touch to create a soft patina. Spray with matte sealer to prevent tarnishing.

broken line

Center Section of Bow Stencil for Country Queen Anne Table

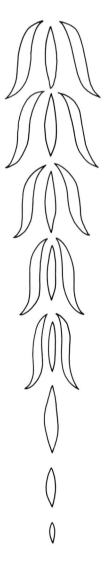

Bell Flower Stencil for Country Queen Anne Table

OCTAGONAL CLOCK

A design reminiscent of one that might be found on an antique Hitchcock chair adds a touch of distinction to the narrow frame of this pretty clock. The gold metallic paint on a flat black background, the moldings, and square outer frame heighten the effect, while a faux tortoiseshell face and mat add their own elegance. Using the clock alone would be lovely. The square frame has been added to permit repetition of the tortoise pattern to pull the design together and make this a very special piece.

The bass wood octagonal clock is purchased separately. Add the numerals and quartz works and use alone or framed, as shown in the photograph.

INSTRUCTIONS

Review checklist (page 16) and assemble

Octagonal Clock

all basic stenciling supplies. Review the materials list for this project.

Sand the clock and prepare for painting. Paint the flat area black and the molding on the sides and around the face gold metallic.

Trace the quarter of the design given on page 99. Fold the paper in half on the broken lines, and trace through the paper to complete one half of the face motif. Cut a stencil from this pattern.

Placing the stencil as indicated in the photograph, paint one half of the design with gold metallic paint, flipping the stencil to paint the second half. Allow to dry. Coat with high-gloss spray glaze.

Following the instructions on page 24, paint a faux tortoiseshell finish on the mat and clockface. The pictured clock shows tortoiseshell with a metallic base coat, but a flat yellow base coat would work just as well. Finish the tortoiseshell with five or six coats of varnish for good depth. When dry, cut the mat to fit the 14″ frame.

If you cannot find a black frame with a gold band, purchase a brown frame and paint it black.

Cut an opening in the center of the mat board for the clockface. Insert the clockface and, following the instructions that accompany the clockworks, assemble the various pieces. Four short screws inserted through the back of the mat into the wood of the octagon will hold everything together firmly. Apply the clock's numerals, insert a battery, and enjoy a beautiful country collectible!

Materials

Octagonal clock (The one pictured is 12″ across.)

14″ × 14″ square frame with gold band at inside edge

Quartz clockworks with hands and numerals

15″ × 15″ heavy art board for mat

Paints

    Acrylic base coat: black

    Classic gold leafing compound

    For faux tortoiseshell, see paint requirements and instructions on page 24.

Final finish: high-gloss spray glaze coat

Stencil for Octagonal Clock

SACHERVILLE TRUNK I: FLEUR-DE-LIS TRUNK

Old trunks of any size and design are among the most desirable of country collectibles. They add charm and atmosphere as well as storage to many rooms. What a bonanza to find that new, unfinished trunks can be bought and finished to look like antiques! In addition, these small trunks are fresh, clean, and sturdy, and there's no need to worry about using them even though they look wonderfully old. Much of the success of the simulated antique look stems from the way the gold leaf has been applied on the borders of the panels. Notice the soft shading.

Though these trunks can be purchased with beautiful moldings on the top and bottom, a few additions can be made to personalize the basic trunk. For example, turn 2″ unfinished hardwood wheels on their sides and glue them to the bottom of the trunk to create bun feet. Dollhouse molding finished with gold leaf can be used to outline the faux tortoiseshell panel on the lid of the trunk, adding elegance and interest.

Although the instructions below are for a specific trunk, keep in mind that these basic ideas may be easily adapted for any shape trunk of a fairly similar size. The size of the designs can be altered by copier, and the frames around the panels are so straightforward that they can be redrawn, if necessary, to fit another box.

To illustrate the versatility of these designs, two identical trunks have been painted in the same colors but with different designs inside the basic gold-panel borders. The same treatment has been used for the lid of each box, but many other combinations are possible.

INSTRUCTIONS

Review checklist (page 16) and assemble all basic stenciling supplies. Review the materials list for this project (page 103).

Sand, clean, and prepare the trunk and lid for painting. If the trunk is new wood, finish overall with two coats of primer, sanding and rubbing gently with steel wool after each coat is thoroughly dry. Apply two coats of the bright aqua base coat to the inside of the box and the raised inner side of the lid. When the aqua paint is dry, thin the antiquing solution with an equal amount of extender. With a brush or sponge, coat the aqua paint with this mixture. Starting in the area where the antiquing was first applied and using a soft, lint-free rag, rub the surfaces to highlight the centers of the panels.

Measure 1¼″ from the outside edges of the top of the lid and draw a line marking a border around what will be the tortoiseshell panel. (This panel can also be attractively finished like the side panels or with antique aqua, echoing the inside of the box.)

Following the instructions for faux tortoiseshell on page 24, finish the lid panel.

Glue the flat sides of the wheels to the base of the trunk, placing them at the edges but not protruding beyond them. Paint the borders of the lid and the body and feet of the trunk with two coats of flat black paint. Paint the moldings and the dollhouse trim with the gold leaf.

Fleur-de-Lis Trunk

Color Print for Fleur-de-Lis Trunk

Glue the dollhouse molding to the outside edges of the faux tortoiseshell panel on the lid, cutting it with a single-edge razor blade to miter the corners.

Trace the Sacherville border (#8, page 29) and cut one stencil from the pattern. Using the gold leaf paste, paint the border along the top edge of the inside of the trunk, spacing it to fit. Also with gold, stencil the border on both the aqua and the black on the inside of the lid, as shown in the photograph.

Trace the border only of the Leaves and Berries design (pages 106 and 107). Spray the four little cut-outs and the large cut-out with adhesive, and place them on the front and side panels. Stencil the uncovered borders with the gold paste. Keep the application heavier close to the cut-outs, shading it softly toward the edges and corners. Use the fleur-de-lis pattern for the inside of the panels. Enlarge or reduce the size of the design to fit the sides (or to customize for another trunk) by copier as explained in "The Basics" (page 18). Note that the stencil has been inverted and that only the bottom portion is used to create the motif that fills the space between the two fleur-de-lis on the front panel.

Spray the trunk, inside and out, several times with glaze coat. A glossy finish will be shiny and bright, and matte finish will produce a much older look.

Fleur-de-Lis Stencil

SACHERVILLE TRUNK II:
LEAVES AND
BERRIES TRUNK

F ollow the instructions for Sacherville Trunk I (page 100) until it is time to add the stencil design to the side and end panels. Then use the Sacherville Trunk II designs and paint with the gold-paste leafing compound.

Color Print for Leaves and Berries

Leaves and Berries Trunk

End Panel

Front Panel

center

COUNTRY BEDROOM

A restful country decorating theme is both delightful and appropriate for use in a bedroom. This one, with its pale-peach carpet and even paler peach paint under the chair rail, is given a touch of whimsy and color through the use of an adaptation of a historic willow tree and a flowing country floral border which winds around the room just above the chair rail. A hand-netted canopy, an old quilt on the bed, museum document fabric for curtains and dust ruffle, lots of samplers, and a primitive painting commissioned for the room finish the scheme.

The combination of three stencil patterns reflecting the way we combine fabric prints adds a very contemporary feeling to this room. Also, while the colors in the stenciling are picked up from the fabrics in the room, none of the design elements are taken from the chintz itself. (That would be another alternative with still another finished look!) The soft coloring and matching of period styles pulls it all together into a very attractive and soothing composition. These are all important points to be considered when planning a room.

The principal colors in this room are peach and cream. The stencil colors used are deeper peach, coral red, green, brown, and a touch of blue. This is a very comfortable and pleasing combination.

INSTRUCTIONS

Review checklist (page 16) and assemble all basic stenciling supplies. Review the materials list for this project.

Begin by planning the basic stencil layout. Then cut and trace the three stencil patterns. Color each following the key for pencil colors. For the purpose of numbering the colors on the tracings for the stencil overlays, the peach and coral-red shades have been denoted as red and pink.

For the Country Bedroom border, you can save some valuable painting, registration and placement time by combining colors on one stencil and lining up the design with the edge of the film. In this way, the edge can serve as a guide for placement above the chair rail. Paint the design in the colors suggested, taking care not to brush colors into adjacent areas designated for other colors.

Country Bedroom Border

Materials
Stencil paints: deep peach, coral red, green, brown, blue

Color Key
1 red
2 pink
4 green
5 blue
9 brown

Stencil for Country Bedroom Border

Country Bedroom Historic Willow and Wall Border

Cut the green and red of the stylized Heart Flower and Leaf Spray on one piece of film. Cut the blue on a separate piece. This will save a lot of registration time. The detail photograph illustrates the way this design is placed on the diagonal to create an overall pattern on one section of wall under the chair rail.

Noting that all the leaves are green, cut two stencils for the Historic Willow tree and place that design in vertical rows as shown. For a custom look, you can also use the willows as a wide border just above the baseboard.

When placing any patterns on a wall, be careful of any markings you make. Guides are necessary but should be placed so they will not be painted over, for marks show through the paint and remain there forever. Use a chalk line as a guide, or mark lightly and erase just before you start painting.

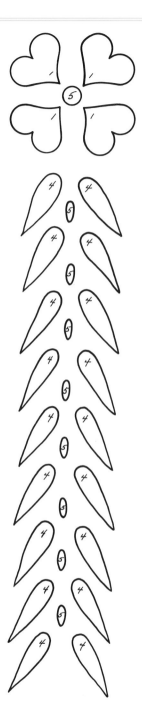

Heart Flower and Leaf Spray

Stencil for Heart Flower and Leaf Spray

Stencil for Historic Willow

Color Print for Historic Willow

CLASSIC PEDESTAL AND WALL BORDER

Photographed in an all-white sun room with floor-to-ceiling windows on three walls, this pedestal was rescued from a garage sale. Fancy molding was added to its top and bottom and, as a final flourish, a Greek Key design was stenciled in gold on the molding. A larger version of the Greek Key design was added to the chair rail, and the result is an elegant classic country setting for wicker furniture and a riot of bright pastel chintz.

The Greek Key motif is a versatile stencil design that can lend special distinction to many a project. For example, the small version shown on the pedestal also has been used on the inside of the Wiltshire Trunk (page 135). A good view of the lid can be seen under the Little Pineapples Trinket Box (page 86).

INSTRUCTIONS

Review checklist (page 16) and assemble all basic stenciling supplies. Review the materials list for this project.

This pedestal can easily be built by a home handyman. It is a tall box 36″ × 14″ × 14″. Wood moldings added to the edges at top and base are commonly found in most lumber stores. The pedestal is finished with several coats of flat white enamel, then stenciled.

For the pedestal, trace the small Greek Key design (#14, page 29), then cut a stencil. Even though it has many bridges, this stencil is quite delicate. Handle it with care and it can decorate an entire room. Position the Greek Key motif on the flat portion of the molding, then stencil the design, using the gold metallic compound.

In the photograph on page 114, the larger Greek Key motif has been stenciled onto a chair rail. Alternatively, it also can be stenciled on a wall.

For the chair rail, trace the design and cut a stencil. Then, leaving a space of about ½″ at both top and bottom, use the gold metallic compound to stencil this short motif. Repeat as many times as necessary.

To use the Greek Key on a wall, draw a light guideline, then stencil the design, repeating it as many times as necessary. Using spray adhesive on the back of the stencil will be very helpful with this design.

Although photographed in metallic gold, this classic motif is equally attractive in other colors.

Materials

Pedestal, box, or wall
Gold metallic compound

Classic Pedestal and Wall Border

Greek Key Stencil for Wall Border

COLLECTION OF SMALL BOXES

COLLECTION OF SMALL BOXES

These wonderful and useful little boxes are very inexpensive, and they offer many opportunities for creative painting and gift-giving. The least costly are the plain round, oval, and heart-shaped Shaker-type boxes that are to be found in every crafts store. Painted gaily, they are very special gift boxes, trinket boxes, or accessories to be used in countless ways. These tiny treasures are to be painted and enjoyed!

Other boxes made from pine and bass-wood are more substantial and available in dozens of shapes and sizes. Anything from a recipe file to a sewing box can be found and enhanced with beautiful stenciling. Use the ideas presented here and the collection of small borders (pages 28 and 29) combined with elements of other stencil designs to create original boxes. Play with color and pattern and hone new stenciling skills on these little projects.

General instructions for all boxes: Sand and clean to prepare for painting. Most new boxes need three coats of the acrylic base coats. These dry so quickly that it is possible to apply successive coats minutes apart if a longer drying time is provided after all three coats have been applied. Stenciling may be done as soon as the paint feels dry, but final varnishing should wait overnight.

ROSEBUD BOX

INSTRUCTIONS

Review checklist (page 16) and assemble all basic stenciling supplies. Review the materials list for this project (page 118).

Prepare and paint the box itself and the top of the lid off-white. Paint the rim of the lid dark green. Allow to dry. Trace the circular rosebud stencil design for the box top, and color it as indicated by the **Color Key**. Cut one stencil for each color. Spray the stencils with adhesive and, after centering the stencil on the top of the box, paint it.

Trace the rosebud border (#4, page 28) and enlarge it to 129 percent of the original. Color this copy to match the box top. Cut three stencils and apply the border around the circumference of the box, placing it as shown in the photograph.

Dry the paint thoroughly, then protect the paint with a coat of spray glaze. A high gloss adds a pretty, porcelainlike finish to this attractive box.

The circular rosebud pattern will also fit nicely on boxes slightly larger or smaller than the one shown. It may also be altered by copier to fit other sizes.

Rosebud Box

Rosebud Stencil for Box Lid

Color Key
1 red
2 pink
4 green

Materials

Unfinished round Shaker-
    type box, 5¼″ in diameter
Paints
    Acrylic base coats: off-
        white, dark green
    Stencil paints: dark green,
        rose, deep rose
Final finish: high-gloss spray
    glaze coat

OVAL BOX WITH GILDED CRANE

INSTRUCTIONS

Review checklist (page 16) and assemble all basic stenciling supplies. Review the materials list for this project.

Prepare the box for painting. Use the deep turquoise-blue for the box and off-white for the lid. Apply as many coats as necessary to completely cover the wood. Dry thoroughly.

Trace the pattern for the box top and cut one stencil. Cut one stencil each for the border (#1, page 28) and for the bush (page 120). With gold metallic compound, stencil the box, placing the designs as shown in the photograph. Dry. Spray with glaze.

This box would also be wonderful painted black and stenciled with gold!

Materials

Unfinished oval box, about 7″ across longest measurement of oval. (Note that the pattern (page 120) is 7″ long and that it can be used equally well on large boxes: The crane will simply be set against a larger background and the motifs around the bottom of the box will be repeated more often.)

Paints

Acrylic base coats: off-white, very deep turquoise blue

Stencil paint: gold metallic compound

Final finish: high-gloss spray glaze coat

Oval Box with Gilded Crane

Bush Stencil for Sides of Box

Stencil for Oval Box with Gilded Crane

RECIPE BOX WITH BUTTERCUP BASKET AND BORDER

INSTRUCTIONS

Review checklist (page 16) and assemble all basic stenciling supplies. Review the materials list for this project (page 122).

If the box you are using is wood, sand if necessary, clean, and paint the lower section blue and the top white. A new box will need two or three coats of paint. Dry well.

Paint can also be applied to a metal recipe box. In this case, sand and paint with one or two coats of white metal primer or with one of the white stain-killing primers. Then apply a coat of white acrylic base coat. Rub gently with steel wool between coats. Follow the stenciling instructions which follow and finish with a protective-spray glaze coat.

Trace the Buttercup Basket stencil design. Because this design is being used as a one-color pattern, only one stencil is needed. Use care in cutting, for the openings are small and many of the bridges are even smaller. Also trace the Buttercup Border (#10, page 29). Again, one stencil is all that is required.

Center the basket design on the lid, and stencil it with navy blue. Using the same blue, stencil the border around the lid, placing it close to the edges. Paint the Buttercup Border around the lower edges of the box with white paint. Dry. Spray with several coats of glaze to provide good protection for an accessory that will be much used and may be splashed in the kitchen.

The blue border on the wall over the countertop is painted with the same blue as the recipe box. This handy little border is very versatile and can also be used along the wall just under the hanging cabinet as well as along the floor just over the baseboard. Space it regularly, allowing about ½″ between motifs.

Recipe Box with Buttercup Basket and Border

Materials

Unfinished wood recipe box
  (standard size:
  5¾" × 3¾" × 3¾")
Paints
  Acrylic base coats: white,
    navy blue
  Stencil paints: navy blue
    and white
Final finish: high-gloss spray
  glaze coat

Color Print for Buttercup Basket

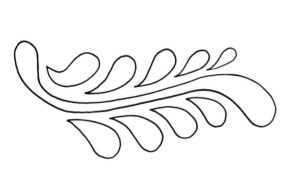

Stencil for Kitchen Border

Stencil for Buttercup Basket

122

MUSTARD AND GREEN OVAL BOX

INSTRUCTIONS

Review checklist (page 16) and assemble all basic stenciling supplies. Review the materials list for this project.

Clean and prepare box for painting. Use the deep-gold base coat for the box, and the dark-green base coat for the entire lid. Allow to dry.

Use the stylized Heart Flower and Leaf Spray design included with the Country Bedroom on page 110. Trace the design, color it, and cut one stencil overlay for each color. Center the heart flower at the front of the box, placing it so that the bottom of the design is about ¼″ from the edge of the box. Paint the flower and the oval berries red and the center of the flower and the leaves green.

For the top of the box, center the heart flower and paint the entire design chamois yellow, repeating as many pairs of leaves as needed to almost reach the far ends of the oval. On the edge of the lid, position the stencil so that just the two hearts and the top spray of leaves are centered. This placement is shown in the photograph. Mask the berries so they won't be painted.

Allow ample drying time, then spray with glaze coat.

This design can easily be used on boxes of many sizes and shapes: The only adjustment to be made is in the number of repeats of the leaf pairs.

> **Materials**
> Unfinished, oval, Shaker-type
>   box, about 6″ across
>   longest measurement
>   of oval
> Paints
>   Acrylic base coats: deep
>   gold, dark green
>   Stencil paints: chamois
>   yellow, bright red, grass
>   green
> Final finish: high-gloss spray
>   glaze coat

Mustard and Green Oval Box

SMALL TRUNK WITH COUNTRY TILE LID

INSTRUCTIONS

Review checklist (page 16) and assemble all basic stenciling supplies. Review the materials list for this project.

Sand the box and prepare it for painting. Glue the small pegs to the bottom of the box to simulate bun feet. Paint the inside of the box and the inside section of the lid pimento red. Paint the exterior of the box, the edge of the inside of the lid, and the feet barn red. Do not paint the edge of the lid or the molding at the bottom edge of the box. Use as many coats of paint as necessary to cover well. Dry.

Directions for painting the top of the lid:
Trace the design for the lid. Following the directions on page 16 and the Color Key, color the tracing. Cut one stencil overlay for each color on the tracing.

After the stencil overlays have been cut, use the colored paper tracing to make a template for painting the lid. Cut out the pointed oval shape on the line outside the yellow border, as indicated on the drawing (page 127). Spray the wrong side of the drawing with adhesive. Center the inner section on the lid of the box. Paint the exposed portion of the lid barn red. Dry. Remove the template.

Next, after protecting the red paint on the outside edges of the lid by covering them with the template, paint the center section off-white. Again, use as many coats of paint as needed. For the pictured box, the yellow border around the stenciled panel was omitted. This border is shown on the color print.

Stencil the color design, using the overlays in sequence and noting that two shades of green and one of yellow denote leaves, but that only one shade of green is needed for stenciling. Stencil the flowers that are shown in pink on the colored tracing with a small amount of the pimento base coat, and

Materials

Small unfinished wood trunk or box. (The dimensions of the trunk in the photograph are approximately 9″ × 5″ × 6″.)

Four small pegs for feet

Paints

    Acrylic base coats: off-white, black, barn red, pimento red

    Stencil paints: pale yellow, medium blue, medium grass green, brown, small amounts of the two red base coats

    Gold metallic paint

    Extender

Black permanent ink marker with fine point

Final finish: high-gloss spray glaze coat

Small Trunk with County Tile Lid

use a small amount of the barn-red base coat for the flowers colored red. Use the color print as a reference for shading.

When the stencil paint is thoroughly dry, outline all elements of the design with the black permanent ink pen. As indicated on the color print, make the outlining irregular to suggest age.

Mix equal amounts of black base coat and extender to make an antiquing solution. With a sponge or brush, apply this solution to the inside of the lid and the outside of the box, taking care to keep it off the unpainted moldings and edge of the box top. Rub off some of the antiquing to highlight the red.

Cut a stencil for the small geometric border (#6, page 28).

Use gold to paint the molding on the bottom edge of the box and the edge of the lid. Also use gold to stencil the geometric border along the upper and lower edges of the box, continuing the pattern around all four sides.

Taking care to use a dry brush, apply an irregular shading of gold on the red border of the lid. Apply the paint more heavily at the edges, feathering it to nothing close to the off-white section. A slightly uneven application is prettiest.

If the colors of stenciled designs seem too bright, mix a small amount of yellow ocher paint with an equal amount of extender to make an antiquing solution. Apply sparingly, then remove most of it, leaving only a film at the center with a slightly heavier coating around the edges.

When dry, spray both lid and box with several coats of high-gloss glaze coat.

Color Print for Country Tile Lid

Color Key
1 red
2 pink
3 yellow
4 green
5 blue
6 light blue
7 light green
9 brown

Stencil for Country Tile Lid

SWEETHEART BOXES

INSTRUCTIONS

Review checklist (page 16) and assemble all the basic stenciling supplies. Review the materials for this project.

Sand the boxes and paint inside and out in a combination of pink and white base coats. The large box is all white except for the rim of the lid; the small box has an all-white lid and a pink bottom section. Any combination of these colors can be used inside. It will take two or three coats of paint to cover the raw wood. Dry thoroughly.

Trace the stencil designs, color the tracings, and cut one stencil for each color on the drawings. Using the pastel stencil paints, paint the tops of the boxes. Note that when the flowers on the small design are cut out and stenciled, the centers will be covered with pink paint. To make the centers yellow, apply small round dots of yellow paint with a watercolor brush.

When the paint has dried, outline the designs with narrow black lines. Use broken lines and keep them light, as shown on the color prints of the designs.

Dry well before spraying with high-gloss glaze coat. To prevent the black ink from bleeding, build up several light coats rather than completely wetting the boxes with glaze.

Materials

Small, unfinished wood heart-shaped boxes (The boxes in the photograph measure 3″ and 4″.)
Paints
  Acrylic base coats: pastel pink, white
  Stencil paints: pastel pink, pastel blue, yellow, green
Black permanent marker pen with fine point (01 nib size)
Final finish: high-gloss glaze coat

Sweetheart Boxes

Color Print for Small Heart

Color Print for Large Heart

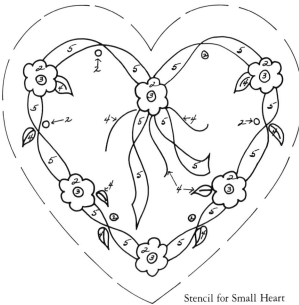

Stencil for Small Heart

Stencil for Large Heart

Color Key
2 pink
3 yellow
4 green
5 blue
6 light blue

129

ANTIQUED TOTE

INSTRUCTIONS

Review the checklist (page 16) and assemble all basic stenciling supplies. Review the materials list for this project.

After cleaning and sanding, paint the inside of the box slate blue, the outside gray. Mask a ¼″ line around each side of the box, as illustrated in the photograph. Mix equal quantities of the very pale-blue stencil paint, extender, and thickener. Paint the ¼″ band around the box, then rub off most of the color so that the base paint shows through. Dry.

Cut a stencil for the little schoolhouse. Save the window cut-out and center it in the appropriate opening to mask that area when painting. Lay the tote flat on a piece of tracing paper and draw the outline of the sides, following the edges with a pencil to make a pattern. Cut two stencils for the lattice: one for the cross sections colored red, one for the orange. Repeat the lattice to fill the sides of the tote. Do not use the frame shown around the lattice on page 132. Trace the tiny apple and make a stencil for it.

Do all stenciling with the very pale blue-gray paint. Place the lattice pattern on the sides of the box with an apple centered in each full diamond and in any others that are more than half complete.

Center the schoolhouse on the front of the box, with the lower edge about ¼″ from the edges of the antiqued border. Place the window cut-out in the appropriate opening and paint. Lay the lattice pattern stencils on the front of the box and, masking off the schoolhouse where the lattice and schoolhouse meet, paint the lattice background. Place an apple on each side of the building as a shrub. Repeat on back of box.

After drying well, spray with matte-finish sealer.

Materials

Wood tote box, about 6″ × 6″ × 10″
Paints
    Acrylic base coats: slate blue, medium gray
    Stencil paints: very pale blue gray
    Extender
    Thickener
Masking tape, ¼″ wide
Final finish: spray matte-finish sealer

Antiqued Tote

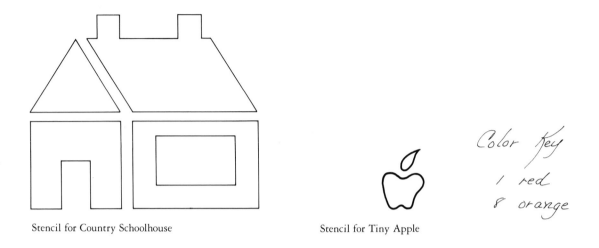

Stencil for Country Schoolhouse

Stencil for Tiny Apple

Color Key
1 red
8 orange

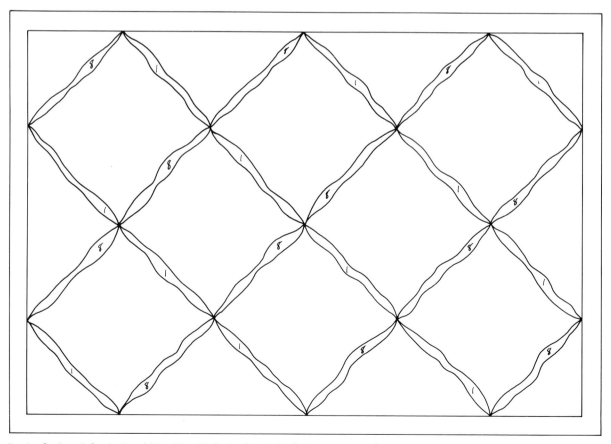

Lattice for Stencil for Antiqued Tote (Use this lattice for the Cards shown on page 40.)

COUNTRY FOLK ART

WILTSHIRE TRUNK

Lined with a handsome coat of pimento-red paint and bordered in dark green with the Greek Key design, this sturdy hardwood trunk sits by the fireplace holding special toys at Grandma's house, but it could just as easily contain the winter's supply of yarn or a stock of magazines. Painted with adaptations of eighteenth-century designs and in the dark colors often found on old boxes, this trunk has a primitive air without looking like a reproduction of an antique. The addition of feet made from hardwood wheels found in a crafts store adds a final touch to the kind of painting that is just right for this trunk.

INSTRUCTIONS

Review checklist (page 16) and assemble all basic stenciling supplies. Review the materials list for this project.

Sand the trunk and clean to prepare for painting. Apply several coats of pimento red to the inside of the trunk and the underside of the lid. Paint the rest of the trunk dark green. Paint the 2″ wheels red, the 4″ wheels green.

Trace the Greek Key design (#14, page 29). Cut one stencil. With a small amount of the dark-green paint, stencil the border around the top of the inside of the trunk and around the underside of the lid, as shown in the photograph.

Use the eighteenth-century floral design on each end of the trunk, centering it in the space. The Pomegranate and the Acorn and Rose designs should be placed on the front and back of the trunk as well as on the top of the lid (see photograph). Center the Acorn and Rose, then add the Pomegranate at each end.

Trace the Acorn and Rose design, coloring the tracing to match the colors indicated in the Color Key. Cut one stencil for red, one for yellow. When cutting the red stencil, save the cut-outs for the flower centers and the large diamond that forms the center of the design.

Materials

Wood trunk, old or new, about 21″ × 12″ × 12″

Eight unfinished hardwood wheels, four 2″ in diameter and four 4″ in diameter

Paints
   Acrylic base coats: forest green, pimento red
   Stencil paint: gold
   Antiquing solution: country blueing
   Extender
   Gold metallic leafing compound
   Final finish: spray matte-finish sealer

Wiltshire Trunk

Eighteenth Century Floral Stencil for Wiltshire Trunk

Pomegranate Stencil for Wiltshire Trunk

Paint the gold areas first, using the stencil cut for the yellow portions of the design and placing as described (page 134). Position the diamond cut-out in the open center and the flower centers in the flowers in order to protect those areas from paint. Next, paint the red areas, centering the stencil over the gold just painted.

Trace the eighteenth-century floral design, color it, and cut one stencil for the red portions, one for the yellow. Use red and gold paint again. Center the stencil on each end of the trunk.

Trace the Pomegranate design, color the copy, and make one stencil for each color. Place the design on the trunk as described above and paint. For the moment, do not worry about the cross-hatching in the flower: add those lines

with a fine brush and green paint after the gold has dried. When the gold (yellow) stencil is cut, save the three cut-outs and use them to mask those spots when the red is painted.

Using the scalloped border (#12, page 29) and gold paint, paint a border on the top of the trunk lid and around the top and bottom edges of the box itself, as shown in the photograph.

Weaken the country blueing antiquing solution by adding about a third of extender. With a small sponge, apply this solution to the trunk and lid. Beginning at the point at which the solution was first applied, wipe off some of the color. Highlight the centers of the panels and the stenciled areas. Dry. Spray with matte-finish sealer.

center

Acorn and Rose Stencil for Wiltshire Trunk

COUNTRY CANDLE SCONCE

A pair of these wonderful sconces would be lovely over a fireplace or sideboard, their candles adding the glow of country comfort to a room. A new piece sculpted from basswood in a very traditional shape, the sconce shown in the photograph is a beautiful foil for gilded stenciling. The traditional qualities of the spray design used on this piece also make it an attractive decoration for the panel of a chest, armoire, or cabinet. Used on the sconce in only one color, the design can be separated, as shown on the drawing, into three or four colors for a startlingly different look.

Meagan's Little Cabinet (page 46) uses two additional designs that can be used with this spray for other projects. Meagan painted her design in pink, green, and gold to illustrate the surprising difference a change in coloring can make.

Materials
Sconce, new or old, about 15″ tall and 4½″ wide
Paints
    Acrylic base coat: colonial blue
    Gold metallic compound
Final finish: high-gloss spray glaze coat

Color Print for Country Candle Sconce

Country Candle Sconce

INSTRUCTIONS

Review checklist (page 16) and assemble all basic stenciling supplies. Review the materials list for this project (page 139).

After sanding to remove any "fuzzies" on the piece, paint the sconce with three coats of blue base coat. When dry, paint the edges and the rim of the shelf with the gold metallic compound.

Trace both the large floral-spray stencil design and the small spray to be used under the shelf. If you plan to stencil only in the me-

tallic gold as illustrated in the photograph, cut one stencil for each spray.

To stencil the design in the colors of the print shown here, trace the drawings and color the tracing to reflect the colors noted by numbers on the drawing. Cut one stencil overlay for each color.

Spray the cut stencils with adhesive, then paint the design with the gold metallic compound. When dry, spray with high-gloss glaze coat.

Small Floral Spray Stencil for Country Candle Sconce

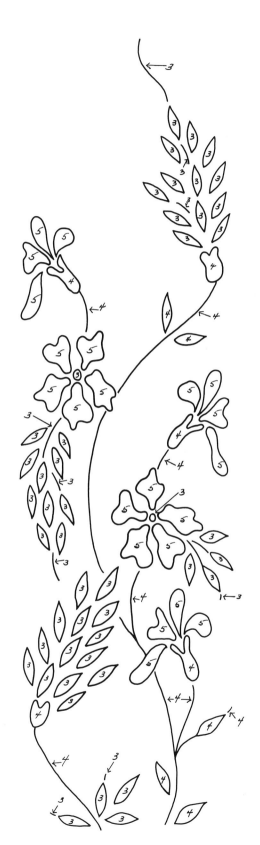

Color Key

3 yellow
4 green
5 blue

Large Floral Spray Stencil for Country Candle Sconce

TAUF-SCHEIN FOOTSTOOL

The treasured family birth record from Pennsylvania dates to 1803, and its lovely colors and delicate design have inspired an interest in the roots and history of the Pennsylvania Fraktur art. Even those not fascinated with the meaning of the various elements in the drawings are drawn to the imagination and beauty of the pieces of art that were routinely painted to commemorate births, baptisms, weddings, deaths, book plates, house blessings, even achievement in school.

The design for the stool top was inspired by the tauf-schein, and it contains the tulip, distelfink (bird), and heart that so often dominate all old paintings. The antiqued paint and the simplified motif on the apron of the stool add to the impression that this might be a copy of a country antique.

To make the stenciling on the stool top more closely resemble the old Fraktur art, which usually outlined objects in black ink, the design painted on the linen has been outlined with a permanent black fabric-marking pen. The lines are faint and broken to heighten the antique look, as shown in the print of the bird.

INSTRUCTIONS

Review checklist (page 16) and assemble all basic stenciling supplies. Review the materials list for this project.

Sand, clean, and prepare the stool for painting. Apply one or two coats of bright aqua flat base coat. The aqua color should be very bright because the blue antiquing will tone it down considerably. Allow time for the paint to dry completely.

Thin the antiquing solution with an equal amount of extender. With a brush or small sponge, coat the stool with the thinned solution. Beginning in the area on which the

Materials

Small footstool (The top of the photographed model measures 13″ × 15″.)
½ yard heavy-weight ecru upholstery linen
Paints for stool
    Acrylic flat-finish base coat: bright aqua
    Antiquing solution: country blueing
    Stencil paint: black
    Extender
Final finish: high-gloss spray glaze coat
Stencil paints for linen cover: antique red, black, country blue, medium green, burnt sienna, bright yellow
Black fabric marker with fine point

Tauf·Schein Footstool

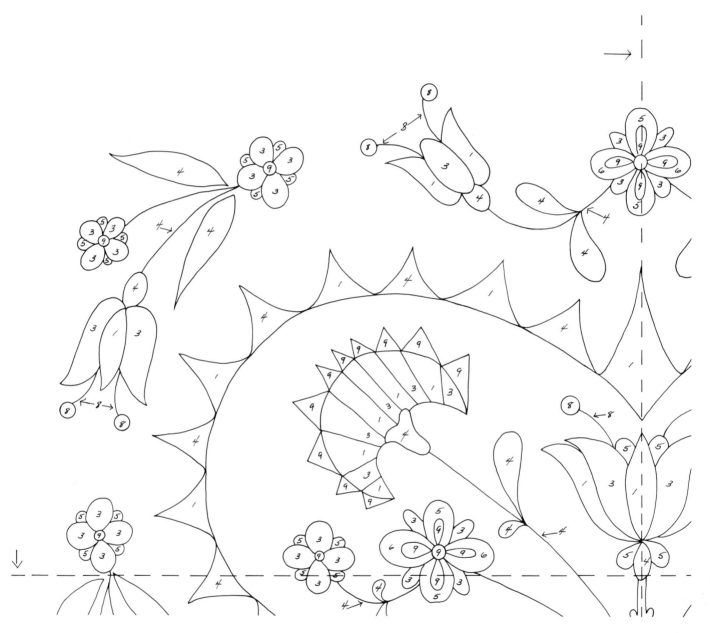

One-Half of Top Stencil for Tauf-Schein Footstool. Match broken lines to folds of tracing paper.

One-Half of Bottom Stencil for Tauf-Schein Footstool. Match broken lines to folds of tracing paper.

Color Key
1 red
3 yellow
4 green
5 blue
6 light blue
8 black
9 brown

Color Print for Tauf–Schein

Color Key
+ green
7 light green

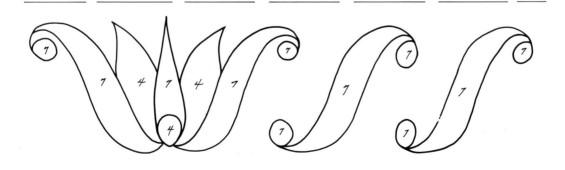

Border Stencil for Tauf–Schein Footstool

solution was first applied, wipe off the antiquing solution with a soft, lint-free rag, leaving the color darker at the edges and near the joints in the wood. Rub to highlight portions of the aprons. Allow to dry.

Trace the border for the stool, color the tracing, and cut one stencil for each of the two colors. With black stencil paint, paint the design on the stool aprons, adding or subtracting the number of scrolls as needed. Dry. Spray with the high-gloss glaze coat to achieve a bright finish.

Cut a piece of linen to fit the stool top, adding at least two inches extra on both the horizontal and the vertical measurements. Wash the linen to remove the sizing. Iron well, then fold the linen in quarters and lightly press the folds to establish markings.

Tauf–Schein Footstool

Fold a large sheet of tracing paper into quarters. Matching the fold lines with the slashed lines on the drawings, trace the design for the stool top. The two drawings, when joined, comprise one half of the complete design. Avoid preparing unnecessary stencils by cutting only one half of the complete design.

Color the tracing, using the Color Key for guidance. Cut one stencil for each color shown on the drawing. (To avoid preparing so many stencils, you can combine the dark-blue, brown, and black colors on one piece of film.)

Next, trace only the smooth outline that defines the shape of the heart and cut a stencil on that line. Include on the stencil film the broken lines that cross the edge of the heart and use these as registration marks, lining them up with the folds of the linen when centering the heart on the fabric. (The heart-shaped stencil will have a large opening without support, but since this stencil will be used only once and just briefly, it will not be a problem.) Center this stencil on the linen and, working with the antique red color, work a shaded line about a half-inch wide inside the heart outline. Make the color darkest at the outline and shade it to nothing at about ½″.

When stenciling, it is best to begin with the red stencil and follow with green, yellow, and then the others. Use the same blue for both light and dark shades of blue on the stencil design. Shade the bird's breast as shown on the color print.

When all painting is complete, outline each motif lightly with the black fabric marker, breaking the lines often to simulate the Fraktur style. Set the color as directed by the paint manufacturer. Mount the fabric on the stool top and replace the top on the base of the stool.

PENNSYLVANIA DUTCH PLACE MAT

T he bright colors of Pennsylvania Dutch Fraktur painting add spice to a textured cotton place mat. On generous-sized, ready-made mats with a fringe trimming, add the stencil design and enjoy this cheerful addition to the breakfast table!

INSTRUCTIONS

Review checklist (page 16) and assemble all basic stenciling supplies. Review the materials list for this project.

Materials
Cotton place mat, natural color
Stencil paints, crayons, or fabric dyes: bright red, cobalt blue, canary yellow, grass green, brown
Black permanent fabric pen with fine point

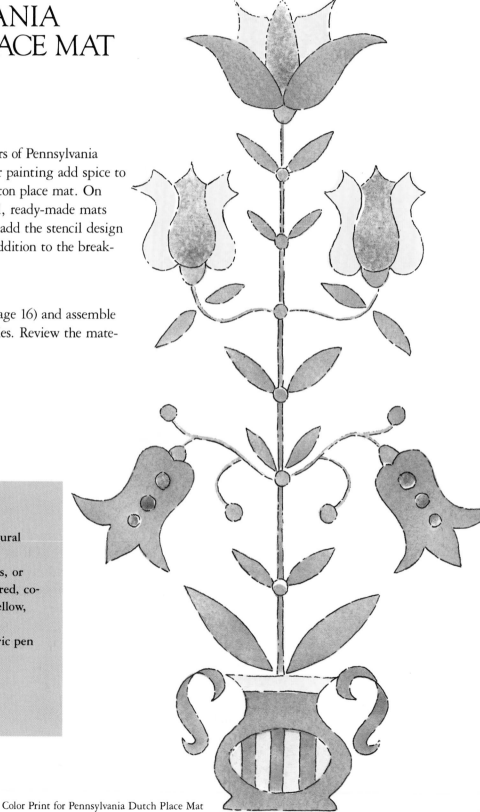

Color Print for Pennsylvania Dutch Place Mat

Pennsylvania Dutch Place Mat

Trace the design and enlarge it by copier to fit your place mat. Because the mat shown in the photograph is 14″ wide, it was necessary to enlarge the stencil design to 118 percent of the original. This leaves a space of 2″ above and below the design.

Color the tracing of the design following the Color Key, and cut one stencil for each color on the drawing. When cutting the large red tulips, first cut the little blue dots and save the cut-outs. Then cut out the tulip. When ready to paint, start with the red stencil, spray the little cut-out dots with adhesive and use them to mask the dots on the flower while applying the red paint. This will leave clean fabric for the application of the blue.

When all colors have been applied and set following the manufacturer's directions, outline the entire design with the black marker to simulate Fraktur art. If desired, use one flower from the design on the corner of a matching napkin or one of contrasting color.

Color Key

1 red
3 yellow
4 green
5 blue
9 brown

Stencil for Pennsylvania Dutch Place Mat

AMISH DOLL BENCH

L ittle girls have always enjoyed doll furniture made especially for them. Today's children are so lucky to have beautiful pieces like this doll bench readily available in crafts and art supply stores. They only need a little paint to make them special. Sturdily constructed, these wood pieces add a custom country look to any doll's home, or they may be used to add a touch of whimsy to a country arrangement of flowers and other collectibles. However you decide to use this or any other small piece, it is fun to add a touch of color and enjoy an endearing miniature.

INSTRUCTIONS

Review checklist (page 16) and assemble all basic stenciling supplies. Review the materials list for this project.

Begin by sanding lightly if necessary, and spraying with a very light coat of clear sealer. Allow to dry. Then rub gently with steel wool to remove any "bubbles" or rough spots.

Trace the two Dutch Tulip designs. Color the tracings and cut four stencils for each design: one for red, one for orange, and one each for green and yellow. The light-green center leaf formation on the larger design may be added to the yellow stencil with no problem.

Although the red is shown on the drawings as red and orange, and green is shown in two shades for the purpose of separating the stencil overlays, only one shade of red paint and one shade of green paint are to be used.

Materials

Small, wood, high-backed bench or other miniature furniture piece. (The bench in the photograph is about 10″ tall and 10″ wide.)

Paints

Stencil paints: red, green, yellow, plus a very small amount of both yellow ocher and brown for an antiquing solution

Extender

Spray sealer

Final finish: high-gloss spray glaze coat

Notice that the little cut-out heart on the back of the bench replaces the flame over the heart on the drawing. It is not necessary to cut the flame portion of the design on the yellow overlay if the project being stenciled has a similar cut-out. For a solid area, use the design as presented.

Spray the wrong sides of the stencils with adhesive. Position the smaller design on the bench seat and the larger design on the back, as illustrated in the photograph. Paint seat, back, and edges using the suggestion below for placing the borders.

Use red paint for the portions of the design shown as red and orange. Work the paint more heavily at the edges, feathering it to nothing at the center so that the yellow paint can be used over raw wood. Paint all the yellow areas with yellow paint and all the green areas with green paint.

For the little heart border shown on the edges of the seat and arms of the bench, use the repeating **heart** border (#2, page 28). Place it horizontally as shown on the edge of the bench seat, but turn the hearts, as illustrated in the photograph, on the vertical edges of the bench. It is not necessary to cut another stencil for such a small job. Just stencil the green, then turn the stencil and place each heart individually.

Allow to dry. To make an antiquing solution, mix equal portions of the yellow ocher and brown stencil paints with double that amount of extender. Test the color on the underside of the bench seat. Adjust if necessary or try another color mixture, perhaps yellow-red-brown. Apply antiquing solution sparingly with a sponge. Wipe off to highlight especially around the colored areas. Dry thoroughly, and spray with sealer for a matte finish or with heavy glaze coat for a bright shine.

Sample of a Stencil

Amish Doll Bench

Color Print for Seat of Amish Doll Bench

Color Print for Back of Amish Doll Bench

Stencil for Seat of Amish Doll Bench. Use this stencil for the interior flat surface of the Small Tray with Dutch Hearts and Tulips (page 156).

Stencil for Back of Amish Doll Bench. Use this stencil for the interior and exterior sides of the Small Tray with Dutch Hearts and Tulips (page 156).

Color Key

1 red
3 yellow
4 green
7 light green
8 orange

SMALL TRAY WITH DUTCH HEARTS AND TULIPS

The exuberant joy in the colors and designs of the Pennsylvania Dutch add a touch of country style to this small, useful tray. The mingling of brilliant gold, red, and green background paints add to the highlights of stenciling and make this tray a treasure to display with other collectibles, while the high-gloss finish makes it a very practical piece to use as intended.

INSTRUCTIONS

Review checklist (page 16) and assemble all basic stenciling supplies. Review the materials list for this project.

Sand the tray, clean, and paint the outside red and the inside gold on the flat surface and dark green on the sides (see photograph).

The stencils for the Dutch Hearts and Tulips are on page 155 with the Amish Doll Bench. For the tray in the photograph, the designs were enlarged to 120 percent of the original. If the tray you are using is slightly different in size, you can either enlarge or reduce the design by copier, or stretch and shorten the borders by altering the lengths of the tulip stems.

Trace the tulip border, enlarge it, and color as suggested. Cut four stencils, one for each color on the drawing. For the design on the interior flat surface, trace the larger Dutch Heart and Tulip design, enlarge it to 120 percent, and color it. Cut four stencils.

Using the stencil colors suggested above and referring to the color print, paint the patterns on the interior flat surface of the tray. Although red is shown as red and orange, and two shades of green are used on the drawing to separate the number of stencils to be cut, use only one color red and one green when painting the design. The colors will appear more muted on the gold background of the tray than on the white background of the color print.

On the dark-green interior sides, paint only the heart and two leaves from the tulip border, making the heart green and the leaves and stems black.

On the red exterior sides, paint the entire tulip border, using yellow for the heart and tulips and black for the leaves, stems, and tulip centers. Repeat the same coloring on the ends of the tray, omitting the heart.

Let the stencil paint dry for several days, then finish with a coat of high-gloss glaze coat.

Materials

Small wood tray with sloped sides, about 9″ × 10″
Paints
  Acrylic base coats: dark green, gold, bright red
  Stencil paints: dark green, bright red, black, gold, blue
Final finish: high-gloss spray glaze coat

Small Tray with Dutch Hearts and Tulips

QUILT SAMPLER AFGHAN

T he simplest of country comforts—a soft, warm afghan in which to snuggle—can be a beautiful, decorative addition to a keeping-room or den. Miniaturized quilt motifs for stencil patterns create the effect of appliqué or cross-stitch very quickly.

Several companies import afghan fabrics in various colors and weaves. Designed basically for cross-stitch, most of these fabrics are made with an even-weave construction with different thread counts, and many are woven with a block pattern divided by strips which create a pattern rather like a quilt joined with sashing or lattice strips. These make ideal fabrics for stenciling. The afghan shown in the photograph has blocks that (including the tiny diamond pattern that outlines the blocks) are approximately five inches square.

By altering the size of the stencil designs and perhaps changing the layout, you can use fabric with larger or smaller blocks for your own afghan. (See page 18 for guidance in making these easy adjustments.) The prettiest background colors for this project are cream, ecru, and white. Add the bright colors with paint.

INSTRUCTIONS
Review the checklist (page 16) and assemble all basic stenciling and sewing supplies. Review the materials list for this project.

NOTE: Most afghan fabrics are woven about 45″ wide. Purchase enough yardage to cut a square and allow for fringe. For the afghan shown in the photograph, half a square on one side was removed to make the fringe and create a square six blocks long and six blocks wide.

Save any cut-off fabric for practice to improve your dry-brush technique and to make certain that the paint or dye you choose does not bleed into the fabric. Treat the test sample as instructed on the paint package to set the color, then wash the sample several times to check washability.

Following the even weave, stitch around the afghan fabric on the line at which the fringe will end. A small zigzag stitch is ideal, but a straight stitch will do if a machine with a zigzag stitch is unavailable. Pull out the horizontal threads on all four sides to create a self-fringe. Gently wash the fabric to remove any sizing. Dry and press well.

Materials
White even-weave acrylic afghan fabric (see note)
Fabric stencil paints or dyes: phthalo blue, yellow ocher

Size: 44″ × 44″, excluding fringe

Quilt Sampler Afghan

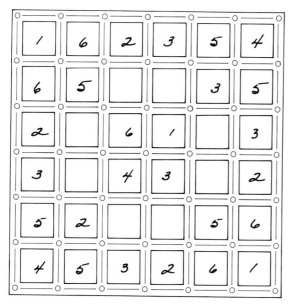

Quilt Layout

LAYOUT DRAWING

The numbers in the squares correspond to those on the six quilt square designs. Distribute them as suggested or plan another layout, using all or some of the designs. The small circles indicate the positioning of the flower from the President's Wreath pattern (#1, page 161). The lines indicate the positioning of the small diamond border in the lattice strips.

Trace the six miniature quilt designs, and cut one stencil for the portions of design shown in blue and one for those shown in yellow.

Following the numbers in the layout drawing (pages 160–163) or using an arrangement of your own, stencil the miniature quilt designs, centering them in the individual blocks. Each miniature quilt block has been identified by its traditional name and a number. The small circles on the layout indicate that a flower from the President's Wreath #1 is to be centered in that portion of the sashing.

Fix the paint or dyes by following the manufacturer's instructions on the package.

Color Key

3 yellow

5 blue

Stencil for President's Wreath #1

Stencil for Pomegranate #2

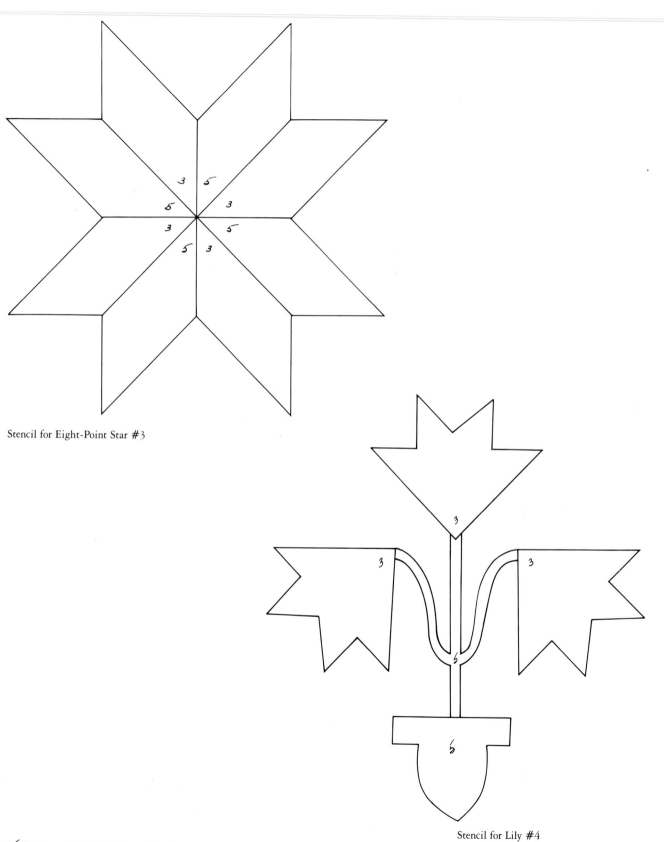

Stencil for Eight-Point Star #3

Stencil for Lily #4

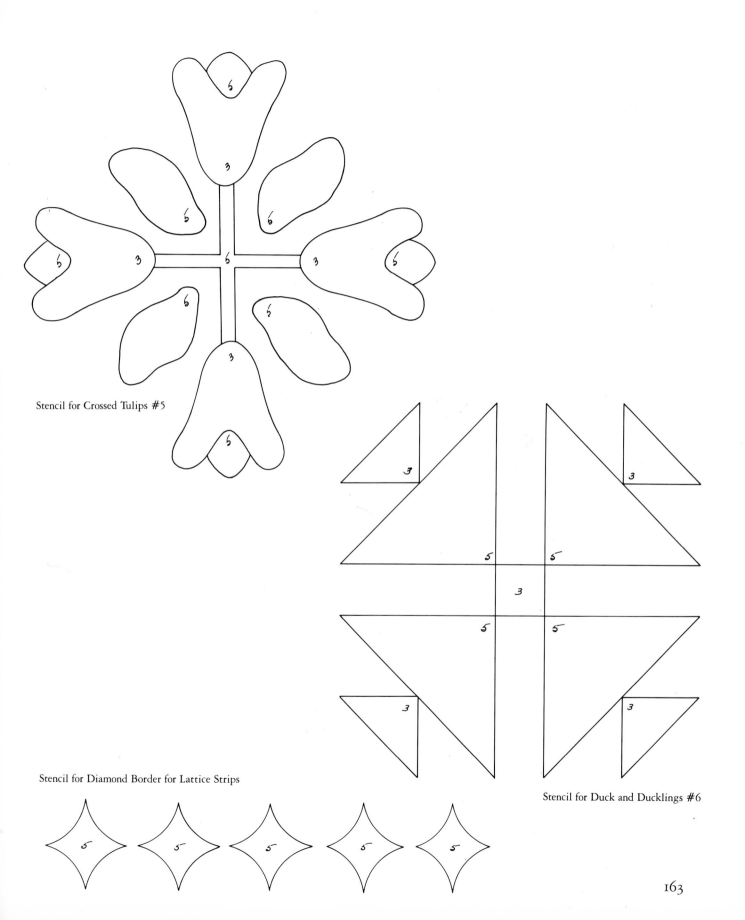

Stencil for Crossed Tulips #5

Stencil for Diamond Border for Lattice Strips

Stencil for Duck and Ducklings #6

SHAKER HANGING RACK

The Shaker tradition of combining beauty with utility is beautifully exemplified in this rack with four pegs. This is a five-inch-wide board into which four holes have been drilled for the gracefully carved Shaker pegs. Beveled edges are an elegant detail. To reveal the grain to best advantage, the wood has been finished with white pickling, an interesting background for stenciled design.

As shown in the photograph, this rack makes a lovely accessory in a little girl's room to display a favorite hat and dress. Many collectors like to use this kind of rack to display antique clothing since it can be finished so easily to look like an original.

INSTRUCTIONS

Review checklist (page 16) and assemble all basic stenciling supplies. Review the materials list for this project (page 166).

Although this rack was handmade by a dear friend especially for this book, similar racks may be purchased at fine crafts and hobby stores. The stencil can be repeated or stretched to fit most racks. The spaces between pegs on this rack are 9¼″ on center. If your rack is shorter, you can place the leaf spray so that its ends are closer together at the tops, or you can reduce the design by copier to fit your particular needs.

Finish the unpainted wood rack by sanding and applying one coat of clear sealer. Mix

Heart and Vine Stencil for Shaker Hanging Rack

Color Key
1 red
3 yellow
4 green

Shaker Hanging Rack

Color Print for Shaker Hanging Rack

and apply the white pickling solution following the instructions on page 23.

Trace the Heart and Vine design. Color the tracing to match the colors suggested in the Color Key. Cut one stencil overlay for the heart, and combine the yellow and green on another piece of film.

Centering the hearts between the pegs, stencil the design onto the rack. Reverse the stencil to paint the other side of the vine.

If a second finishing coat is desired, allow the stencil colors to dry overnight before applying clear varnish. This second coat can be either matte finish or high gloss, as you prefer.

Materials

Wood rack similar to the one
   shown, about 36″ long
Paints
   Clear varnish or sealer
   White oil-base enamel or
     white pigment
   Mineral spirits
   Boiled linseed oil
   Stencil paints: deep rose,
     olive green, gold
Final finish: clear varnish

INDEX

All of us at Meredith® Press are dedicated to offering you, our customer, the best books we can create. We are particularly concerned that all of the instructions for making the projects are clear and accurate. We welcome your comments and would like to hear any suggestions you may have. Please address your correspondence to Customer Service Department, Meredith® Press, Meredith Corporation, 150 East 52nd Street, New York, NY 10022.

For information on how you can have *Better Homes and Gardens* delivered to your door, write to: Mr. Robert Austin, P.O. Box 4536, Des Moines, IA 50336.